THE VALLEY OF THE KINGS - THE VALLEY OF THE QUEENS

LUXOR

BONECHI

INDEX

LUXOR

A strip of green in the midst of yellow desert, cultivated fields against a background of red rocks (the Libyan Chain), this is the setting for Luxor, once one of the greatest capitals of the ancient world. And it is still a captivating city, with its modern hotels lining the banks of the Nile, the feluccas gliding over the tranquil waters of the river, and the small silent streets of the bazaar coming to life towards evening with colour, light and noise.
This is the ancient, great city of Thebes, capital of the Egyptian empire for almost a thousand years, called by Homer in the ninth canto of the Iliad "the hundred-gated Thebes," where "only the grains of sand of the desert surpassed the quantity of riches enclosed within". The Copts called it Tapé, hence the Greek *Thebai*, but for the Egyptians it was *Uaset*, "the dominant," and *Niut*, "the City", later known as *Diospolis Magna*. Its present name, Luxor, derives from the Arabic *Al-Uqsur*, a translation of the Latin *castra* - in fact, the Romans maintained two encampments in the city. In the Memphite period, it was a small village, a site for worship of the war god Munt, whose temples marked the boundaries of the ter-

The temple of Amun-Ra and, below, the white sails of feluccas along the Nile at Luxor.

The architectural diversity of the temple of Amun-Ra can best be appreciated from the Nile. Near to the temple is the old "Winter Palace Hotel" built in Victorian style in 1886. Many famous personalities, writers, archaeologists, politicians and members of the royal families of Europe have stayed here.

ritory. During the 10th Dynasty its importance grew thanks to its geographical position and for political reasons, and the military successes of its princes eventually succeeded in making it a power. The capital of the pharaohs' during the New Kingdom, the great god Amun was worshipped here with much ceremony as part of the triad with Mut and Khonsu. This was the era of great victories and triumphs in Anterior Asia, in Nubia, and in Libya. It was perhaps the most felicitous of periods in Egyptian history and Thebes had no rivals: the victorious pharaohs accumulated incredible wealth ("the city where the houses are rich treasuries") from war spoils. Merchants arrived from the Red Sea, the Persian Gulf, and even from the Sahara, via the oases routes, to make their fortunes, as well as those of the inhabitants of Thebes, who, it is said, reached the incredible number of half a million in that period.

The temples, the dwellings of the gods, rose on the east bank of the river; buildings for the cult of the dead sovereigns rose on the west bank. Beyond this row of temples, running parallel to the river, is the imposing rock bluff which hides the Valley of the Kings. Then, as inexorable for Thebes as for other cities, came decline. The geographical position that a thousand years earlier had favoured its rise to power now became the prime factor in its isolation: too far from the centre of activity around the Delta, where the Ramessides were forced to create military posts to stem the foreign invasions, Thebes lost its political, spiritual, and military supremacy.

The dynasties that followed came from the Delta, and the cities of Tanis, Bubastis, and Sais took Thebes' place as capital of Egypt. Left defenceless, Thebes fell prey to the Assyrian army lead by Assarhad-don, which sacked

it in 672 BC and again in 665, while Assurbanipal's army deported the townsmen to use them as slaves and stripped the town of its statues and treasures.
By the Ptolemaic era, Thebes had become a provincial backwater. During the Ptolemaic period, the city rebelled against Roman oppression but the insurrection failed and the city was razed by Cornelius Gallus. In the centuries that followed, the original significance of the architectural structures was completely lost and many were demolished to build over or beside the temples. But the disappearance of Thebes coincided with the growth of Luxor which gradually developed into a vacation spot for the new tourists, the winter residence of rich Europeans who were intrigued by the civilization that was emerging from the desert sands.
Today Luxor is constantly expanding, with an increasing number of modern hotels, easy berthing for the attractive Nile cruise ships and a newly-made golf course. Luxor is now one of the most pleasant destinations for a holiday in Egypt.

Above, an archaeological excavation at Thebes in a photograph taken in January 1881.

Left, a group of American tourists from a Mediterranean cruise boat visit the temple of Luxor in April 1923.

Left, the two colossal statues of Ramesses II at the entrance to the temple. In the two smaller photos, columns with closed papyrus columns and bundled papyrus columns with closed capitals.

The Temple of Amun-Ra

The only evidence of Luxor's glorious past is the temple built by the ancient Egyptians to the glory of Amun-Ra, king of the gods, and which they called by the name of Southern Harem of Amun. The temple, uncovered in 1883 by Gaston Maspero, is 260 metres long and was mostly built by two pharaohs, Amenhotep III, who began it in the 14th century BC, and Ramesses II, who completed it by adding the great porticoed court with its axis shifted eastwards, unlike the rest of the structure which lies north-south. The architect was probably Amenophis, son of Hotep.
The Temple of Luxor was linked to that of Karnak by a long *dromos* or processional avenue paved in stone and flanked by human-headed sphinxes. This street has not yet been fully excavated and work is continuing to uncover it completely. The avenue ended at the

The magnificent pylon of the temple of Amun-Ra with the statues of Ramesses II and the surviving obelisk of the two that originally stood in front of the statues.

A detail of the long avenue of sphinxes which linked the temple of Luxor to the temple of Karnak in ancient times.

entrance to the Temple of Luxor, at the *Great Pylon* built by Ramesses II. Its 65-metre façade is decorated with bas-reliefs of scenes from the pharaoh's military campaigns against the Hittites.
Originally, the Great Pylon was preceded by two *obelisks*, two *seated colossi*, and four *standing colossi*. Today, only the left obelisk, 25 metres high, is still standing: its "twin" was taken to Paris in 1833 and erected by the engineer Jean-Baptiste Apollinaire Lebas in Place de la Concorde on 25 October 1836. The two granite colossi, fifteen and a half metres in height on bases about a metre high, represent the pharaoh seated on a throne. Of the other four pink granite statues set against the pylon, one represented queen Nefertari and another, on the right and in poor condition, her daughter Merit-Amun.
Having passed through the triumphal entrance, one enters the court of Ramesses II, with its double row of columns with closed papyrus capitals and statues of Osiris between the columns. To the northwest of the courtyard one can admire the temple-deposit of the sacred boats built by Tuthmosis III and dedicated to the triad of Amun, Mut and Khonsu. Next follows a colonnade of two rows of seven bell-shaped columns 52 metres long that leads to the second courtyard, or courtyard of Amenhotep II, which is surrounded on three sides by two rows of closed papyrus columns, like a real and highly evocative forest. From here, across a transversal hypostyle hall, one enters the last sanctuary, the most intimate and sacred part, which gave the temple its name - "Adytum of the south" – where the final moment of the festival of Opet, the largest and most solemn held during the year, was performed.
The festival, which lasted just over fifteen days, started on the nineteenth day of the second month of the flood, generally towards the end of August. The highlight of the ceremony came when the sacred boat of Amun-Ra emerged from the temple of Karnak, carried by thirty priests and followed by the sacred boat of Mut and Khonsu, passed along the avenue of sphinxes and arrived at the temple of Luxor; here the boats were closed in the sanctuary for several days before returning to the temple of Karnak, again accompanied by a joyful crowd singing and dancing.

On the left, the monumental head of a smiling Ramesses II and below, the court of Ramesses II.

This page, above, the obelisk and façade of the temple of Amun-Ra as they are today and how they were seen by David Roberts, with the two colossi buried up to their shoulders by the sand.

The colonnade of the Amenhotep III courtyard showing the bundled papyrus columns and capitals.

This impressive statue of the seated pharaoh, his hands resting on his knees and royal insignia, is in the courtyard of Ramesses II. He wears the nemes headdress and the double crown, symbolic of the two kingdoms united, and an artificial beard.

On the back of this statue is a complex arrangement of hieroglyphs with the name of the pharaoh enclosed in a cartouche.

The first courtyard, named after Ramesses II and the façade of Tuthmosis III's temple.

Two views of the courtyard of Ramesses II, with the Osiris statues of the pharaoh between the columns.

A boy climbs on the half-buried statue of Ramesses II in a photo taken in 1947.

RECONSTRUCTION OF THE TEMPLE OF AMUN-RA

1 - Avenue of Nectanebo I
2 - Obelisks of Ramesses II
3 - Colossi of Ramesses II
4 - First pylon of Ramesses II
5 - Courtyard of Ramesses II
6 - Colonnade of Amenhotep III
7 - Courtyard of Amenhotep III
8 - Vestibule
9 - "Room of the Divine Birth"
10 - Sanctuary
11 - Chapels
12 - Landing

One of the Osiris statues of Ramesses II, the colonnade of Amenhotep III with the open papyrus capitals, and the courtyard of Amenhotep III, where both the shafts of the columns and the capitals are bundled.

The temple of Luxor is also extremely well decorated. There are many beautiful groups of statues representing both gods and pharaohs. On the right, Ramesses II is seen in an attractive group made from limestone, first on his own and then beside a damaged statue of a queen.

On the architectural level, the temple of Amun-Ra represents an amazing range of styles and structures. There are many different kinds of columns, shafts and capitals, such as the rounded columns with open papyrus capitals, seen on the left, and the bundled columns with closed capitals on the right, standing proudly in the courtyard of Amenhotep III.

Museum of Ancient Egyptian Art

Opened in 1975 in an attractive position on the Nile Corniche, this Museum displays countless interesting items relating to the history of ancient Thebes. The works on display are all of great importance, mostly dating back to the 18th Dynasty. Found in excavations in the area of Thebes, they provide eloquent evidence of the city's historic and artistic grandeur. In the garden stand a *statue of Amenhotep II* from Qurna and a *stele* of him from Karnak.
One of the most interesting exhibits is the *Wall of the Talatat*, the recomposition of a wall 18 metres long from a temple built by Akhenaton in Karnak subsequently destroyed by his successors.
The 283 sandstone blocks of which it is composed were found used as filling for the ninth pylon of the Temple of Amun in Karnak, originally built of some 6000 blocks. The myriad of small scenes that stud the wall represent work in the fields, craftsmen at work, the beer factory, the pharaoh and queen Nefertiti worshipping the Sun god.
Another outstanding item is the elegant partially-gilded wooden *head* of the goddess Mehet-neret discovered in the tomb of Tutankhamen, as well as a large *sandstone head* with the unmistakable features *of Akhenaton* and a *stone statue of Tuthmosis I* holding the ankh in his hands. Also on the ground floor, the statues from the temple of Amun are exhibited in a specially constructed room. On 22 January 1989, during preliminary excavations in the court of Amenhotep III in the temple of Luxor, a group of twenty-six statues of gods and pharaohs came to light. The statues were in perfect

The "cachette" room where the statues found in 1989 in the temple of Luxor are exhibited. Right, the statue of Amenhotep II from Qurna, situated in the garden in front of the museum, and below, a section of the "Talatat Wall" from the temple of Karnak.

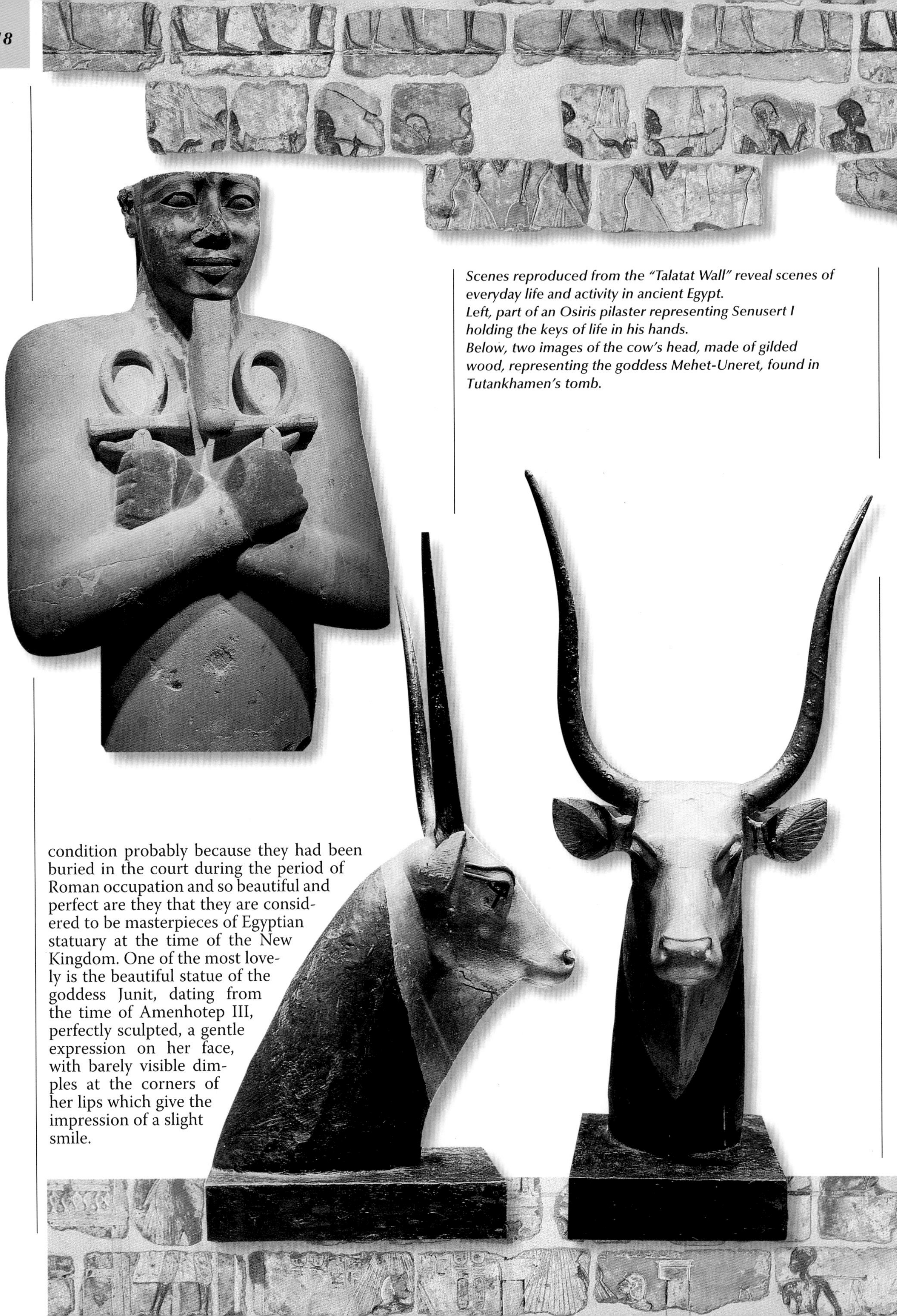

Scenes reproduced from the "Talatat Wall" reveal scenes of everyday life and activity in ancient Egypt.
Left, part of an Osiris pilaster representing Senusert I holding the keys of life in his hands.
Below, two images of the cow's head, made of gilded wood, representing the goddess Mehet-Uneret, found in Tutankhamen's tomb.

condition probably because they had been buried in the court during the period of Roman occupation and so beautiful and perfect are they that they are considered to be masterpieces of Egyptian statuary at the time of the New Kingdom. One of the most lovely is the beautiful statue of the goddess Junit, dating from the time of Amenhotep III, perfectly sculpted, a gentle expression on her face, with barely visible dimples at the corners of her lips which give the impression of a slight smile.

The **Mummification Museum** was inaugurated in Luxor in May 1997. This specialized collection, which complements that of the Egyptian Museum of Cairo with its enormous number of mummies, is indispensable for the country that is foremost in the art of preserving corpses and makes available to the public the most complete information on the subject.
With a specialized *library* and a *multimedia hall* for conferences and projections for visitors, the museum exhibits the most representative archaeological finds relative to the mummification techniques used in ancient Egypt, including a huge *mummified crocodile,* 2.25 metres in length, found in the Temple of Kom Ombo, and the *mummy of Masaharta* son of Pinudjem I, from the period in which this ancient science reached the height of its development (11th century BC). The exhibits are preceded by an area where both the process of mummification and the various phases of the 70-day journey of the dead from the moment of death to that of burial are illustrated and explained.

This gigantic head of Akhenaton was part of the group of enormous statues located in the portico of the solar temple at Karnak.

The statue of the goddess Junit, discovered on 22 January 1989, dates from the time of Amenhotep III. The gentle smile that plays on her lips has earned her the name of the Monna Lisa of Luxor.

The Temple of Karnak

About three kilometres from the Temple of Luxor is the vast monumental area of Karnak, which the Greeks called *Hermonthis.* A mud brick wall divides the archaeological site into three separate areas: the largest is the central area, which Diodorus Siculus tells us was the oldest and which enclosed the dominion of Amun; to the south, still unexplored for about half of its extension (almost nine hectares) and linked to the first by a *dromos* of ram-headed sphinxes, is the dominion of the goddess Mut, wife of Amun and symbolically represented as a vulture; lastly, the dominion of Munt, the god of war, extends to the north over an area of about two and a half hectares.

Each complex changed in size over the course of time and each successive pharaoh left his mark, either by enlarging the temple or by adding rooms and chapels. The structures of the three sacred complexes are identical: the main temple dedicated to the god stands at the centre of each enclosure and alongside is the sacred lake, generally square in shape and used for ceremonies.
The Temple of Amun is the largest columned temple in the world and, as distinguished historians have affirmed, capable of enclosing the entire cathedral of Notre Dame in Paris. So vast is this monument that its

Adorned with a wealth of decorative and architectural detail, the entrance to the temple of Karnak is from the impressive first pylon, preceded by an avenue of sphinxes that originally linked it to the temple of Luxor. Below, the Euergetes Gate and the row of sphinxes with rams heads as they were portrayed by Hector Horeau.

Through the first pylon is a large courtyard, also known as the "Ethiopian Court", 100 metres wide, with rows of seated rams on two sides. The ram was sacred to the god Amun and is seen protecting the pharaoh who is portrayed standing between its front legs.

Below, this statue of a sphinx with a human head stands before the first pylon. Its function was protective and it guarded the entrance to the temples.

complexity provides a valid basis for a study of the evolution of styles, from the 18th Dynasty to the end of the Ramesside era. A short avenue of sphinxes leads to the first pylon (the largest, 113 metres wide and 15 metres thick), the unadorned yet monumental entrance to the temple, dating to the Ptolemaic dynasty. The ram-headed sphinxes represent the god protecting the pharaoh, who is portrayed between the animal's paws.

The *first courtyard*, called the Ethiopian Court, dates to the 22nd Dynasty. It is closed to the north by a portico of robust columns with closed papyrus capitals. Aligned at the feet of the columns are the sphinxes Ramesses II had made to flank the access to the hypostyle hall. At its centre is a tall column with an open papyrus capital; it is all that remains of the gigantic *Pavilion of the Ethiopian King Taharqa*, 21 metres high. In front and to the right of the column is the entrance to the *Temple of Ramesses III*, with Osiris columns around three sides showing the pharaoh in his Jubilee garments.

Set against the second pylon is a damaged colossal granite statue of Ramesses II and another, 15 metres high, representing king Pinudjem. The portal, 29.5 metres high, leads into what is considered one of the most beautiful examples of Egyptian art: the **hypostyle hall**, 102 metres wide and 53 metres long, where some 134 columns, each 23 metres high, rise to the sky. The tops of the open papyrus capitals were about 15 metres in circumference - a veritable forest of columns, and their size and the play of light and shade they create evoke a great sense of wonder. The central nave, begun around 1375 BC by Amenhotep III, who conceived the space as a simple colonnade leading

The temple of Seti II is located in the north-west corner of the great courtyard; the sacred boats were kept in the three chapels dedicated to Amun, Mut and Khonsu.

to the sanctuary of Amun, is higher than the side aisles which were begun by Horemheb, continued by Seti I and Ramesses II, and finally finished under Ramesses IV. This difference in height made it possible to insert the wide openwork stone windows, known as *claustra*, which magically illuminate the interior.
Beyond the hypostyle hall there once stood the obelisks of Tuthmosis I, each 23 metres tall and weighing 143

tons. Hatshepsut's obelisk is still higher (30 metres tall and weighing 200 tons) and for its construction it is said that the queen paid no heed to cost: according to the chronicles of the time, she paid in "bushels of gold as if they were bags of grain."
Beyond the fifth and sixth pylons (respectively of Tuthmosis I and Tuthmosis III), is the unique *Akh-Menu of Tuthmosis III*, the Great Festival Hall also known as the "Temple of Millions of Years." It is a fine hypostyle hall with two rows of ten columns, their shafts painted dark red in imitation of wood, and a row of thirty-two square pillars decorated with various scenes. Scarce traces of 6th century painting have come to light on some of the pillars and reveal that this room was transformed into a church by Christian monks.

The *sacred lake* of Amun's dominion covered an area of 120 by 77 metres and was surrounded by various buildings: the storerooms, the priests' dwellings, even an aviary for aquatic birds. The priests purified themselves in these waters, every morning before beginning the daily sacred rites.
A highly evocative "Open Air Museum" has also been created within the Karnak site, where painted limestone pilasters alternate with a row of statues representing Sekhmet. Here too is the Kiosk of Senusert I, or the "White Chapel", a masterpiece of architecture from the Middle Kingdom with its pure and linear form. It was rebuilt in 1938 with the 77 blocks of limestone from Tura found used as filling inside the third pylon.

A reconstruction of the temple of Amun-Ra on the shores of the sacred lake; the series of pylons and obelisks created an impression of majesty.

The portico of the pavilion of Taharqa, the Ethiopian king of the 25th Dynasty, originally had ten lofty columns, of which only one still survives, with an open papyrus capital.

Ramesses II had a colossal statue built to stand against the second pylon, but it was removed by the High Priest Pinudjem, a pharaoh of the 21st Dynasty. Sculpted between the legs of the colossus is the figure of princess Bent Anat, daughter of Isinophre, one of Ramesses the Great's wives.

To the right of the first court, the courtyard of Ramesses III is particularly fascinating and is a typical example of architecture in the Ramesside period. The pylon, flanked by statues of the pharaohs, leads to a court surrounded by a portico of Osiris pilasters. Following pages, the hypostyle hall, a masterpiece of architecture created under Ramesses II, as it is today and as it was illustrated by David Roberts.

Above, seen from the Amenhotep III court, the beautiful columns of the hypostyle hall soar majestically.
Below, pilasters with an architrave above form the great Festival Hall of Tuthmosis III, the pharaoh's Akh-Menu, his "temple of millions of years". It measured 44 m. by 17 m. and was in celebration not only of his own jubilee, but those of all the pharaohs who had preceded him.

One of the heraldic pilasters of Tuthmosis III, showing the papyrus, symbol of Upper Egypt.

View of the sacred lake. Now highly evocative son et lumière performances take place here.

An Open Air Museum

The excavations and research carried out at Karnak have brought to light amazing monuments and given coherence to an inestimable heritage of objects and remains, only some of which are displayed in the museums of Cairo and Luxor. In time, therefore, the need to provide sufficient and appropriate space to appreciate such a vast and precious wealth of antique treasures without removing them from their original context, became imperative. Thus the idea of an 'open air museum' came into being and now, in this veritable and spectacular "field of stones", long forgotten items and objects that for years had remained in storage were once more brought into the open to be newly rediscovered. One of the loveliest exhibits of this museum is the **White Chapel of Senusert I**, one of the oldest monuments in Karnak, with some of the finest bas-reliefs sculpted in the entire Middle Kingdom. When these remains were discovered during excavations of the third pylon, Henri Chevrier was so greatly impressed by their beauty that in 1938 he decided to work personally on the reconstruction of this sophisticated chapel with pilasters.

The *Chapel of Tuthmosis IV*, consisting originally of numerous monolithic blocks weighing several tons and now standing impressively within the museum, was one of the chapels dedicated to housing the sacred boats that were dismantled by Amenhotep III. Although they were enormous, the various elements that formed the chapel were dispersed or stacked up around the third pylon. For a long period its recomposition therefore seemed to be a task of considerable interest but one that would however, be partial and imperfect. Consequently the definitive and satisfactory rebuilding of the chapel was only completed in 1996.

The "Open Air Museum": a decorated pillar, the White Chapel of Senusert I and the row of statues representing the goddess Sekhmet.

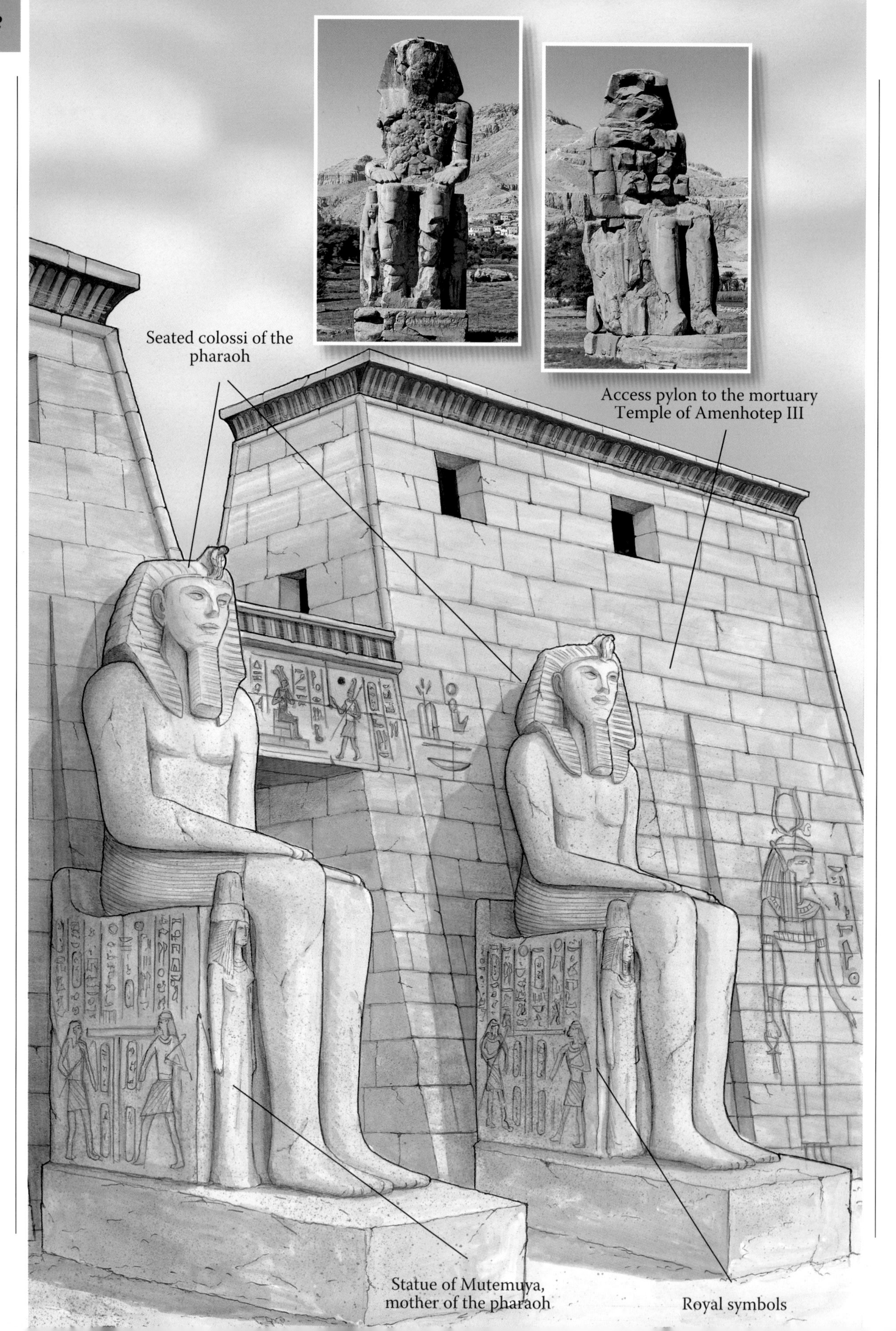
Seated colossi of the pharaoh
Access pylon to the mortuary Temple of Amenhotep III
Statue of Mutemuya, mother of the pharaoh
Royal symbols

The colossi of Memnon

The famous colossi of Memnon are all that remain of the burial temple of Amenhotep III, the magnificence of which is recorded in a stele found by the archaeologist Petrie. These statues, which must have stood on either side of the entrance to the temple, are 20 metres high; their feet alone measure 2 metres in length and 1 metre in width. Cut in monolithic blocks of sandstone, they represent the pharaoh seated on a throne, with his hands resting on his knees. The **southern colossus** is considerably damaged but is in slightly better shape than the other and legend recounts how in 27 BC a terrible earthquake seriously damaged almost all the monuments of Thebes also opening an enormous crack on the colossus from the top halfway to the ground before it toppled over. It was subsequently noted that every morning, at sunrise, the statue emitted a prolonged, indistinct sound, which to some travellers seemed like a sad but harmonious song. Great historians such as Strabo, Pausanias, Tacitus, Lucian, and Philostratus corroborated the fact - and the Greek poets soon turned it into a fine legend. The "singing stone," they said, was Memnon, the mythical son of Aurora and Tithonus, king of Egypt and Ethiopia. Sent by his father to aid Troy, besieged by the Greek army, Memnon killed Antilochus, son of Nestor, in battle, but in turn he fell under the vengeful hand of Achilles. Aurora appealed in tears to Jupiter to have her son resuscitated at least once a day. Thus, every morning, as Aurora caresses her son with her rays, he answers his inconsolable mother with a long, sad lament. Despite the legend, the phenomenon can be scientifically explained. The sounds were caused by vibrations produced on the broken surfaces by the brusque passage from the cold of the night to the warmth of the first rays of the sun.

The Colossi of Memnon, as painted by David Roberts, standing in the flood waters of the Nile.

A view of the Valley of the Kings from above, showing the entrances to the tombs of Tutankhamen and Ramesses VI in the foreground. On the left, the house in the Valley where Carter lived during the excavations.

The Valley of the Kings

Beyond the semi-circle of rocks of Deir el-Bahri lies the valley of the Kings, or *Biban el-Moulouk*, the **Gate of the Kings**. In this ravine, dominated by a cone-shaped mountain often called the "Crown of Thebes," is the necropolis of the great Egyptian sovereigns from the 18th to the 20th Dynasty. The story of the Valley of the Kings begins with the sudden and unexpected decision of Tuthmosis I to separate his tomb from his mortuary temple - and moreover to bury his body not in a showy monument but in a secret, inaccessible place. His chief architect, Ineni, excavated a shaft tomb in a lonely ravine, cut a steep stairway into the rock, and at its bottom built the sepulchre; this plan was followed by all the later pharaohs. Ineni himself has provided us with documentation of the utmost secrecy of the undertaking, in a phrase he had carved into the wall of the mortuary chapel: "I alone oversaw the construction of the rupestral tomb of His Majesty. No one saw anything; no one heard anything." But the repose of Tuthmosis I, like that of most of the pharaohs, was of short duration for even during the period of the pharaohs, despite surveillance by teams of guards by day and night, systematic plundering of the tombs occurred and the precious tomb furnishings were removed. One of the objects most coveted was the so-called "heart scarab", the amulet placed on the mummy over the heart to permit the deceased to save himself on the day of judgement, when his actions were weighed. Yet these kings, so powerful in life, were destined not to find peace in death. During the Ramesside period, the priests of Amun lost their ancient authority. They nevertheless remained devoted to their deceased kings, and in order to ensure them an undisturbed afterlife and to avoid profanation of the tombs, began transporting the royal mummies from one burial site to another. These transferrals were so frequent that Ramesses III was buried all of three times! Finally, they decided to prepare a practically inaccessible secret hiding place: in the mountain of Deir el-Bahri, they had a shaft dug to a depth of about twelve metres. A long corridor led off from the bottom of the shaft into a spacious room. At night and in great secret, with only a few torches to provide light, as stealthily as the tomb raiders themselves, the priests took the pharaohs from their sarcophagi in the Valley and laid them all to rest in this

The numbering of the tombs

It was the Egyptologist, John Gardner Wilkinson, who decided to number the tombs in the valley and to carry out the chronological cataloguing of the pharaohs who are buried there. In 1827, Wilkinson assigned a progressive number to each tomb by painting it on the entrance or on nearby rock. He began numbering with the tomb lowest down in the Valley (that of Ramesses VII, No. 1) and proceeded along the main path, numbering as he went on both the left and the right. All the tombs bear the abbreviation KV for King's Valley and this is followed by the progressive number. Altogether 62 tombs were recognized and numbered, until on 6 February 2006 a new tomb was discovered, situated in the centre of the Valley between KV10 (Amenmose) and KV62 (Tutankhamen). The funerary chamber contained five wood sarcophagi, inside which were mummies with coloured funerary masks, dating from the 18th Dynasty.

A photograph of the Valley taken not long after the discovery of Tutankhamen's tomb. Beside the white tent traces of Carter's excavations can be seen. The famous English archaeologist is seen in this portrait, an oil painting possibly by his father, Samuel.

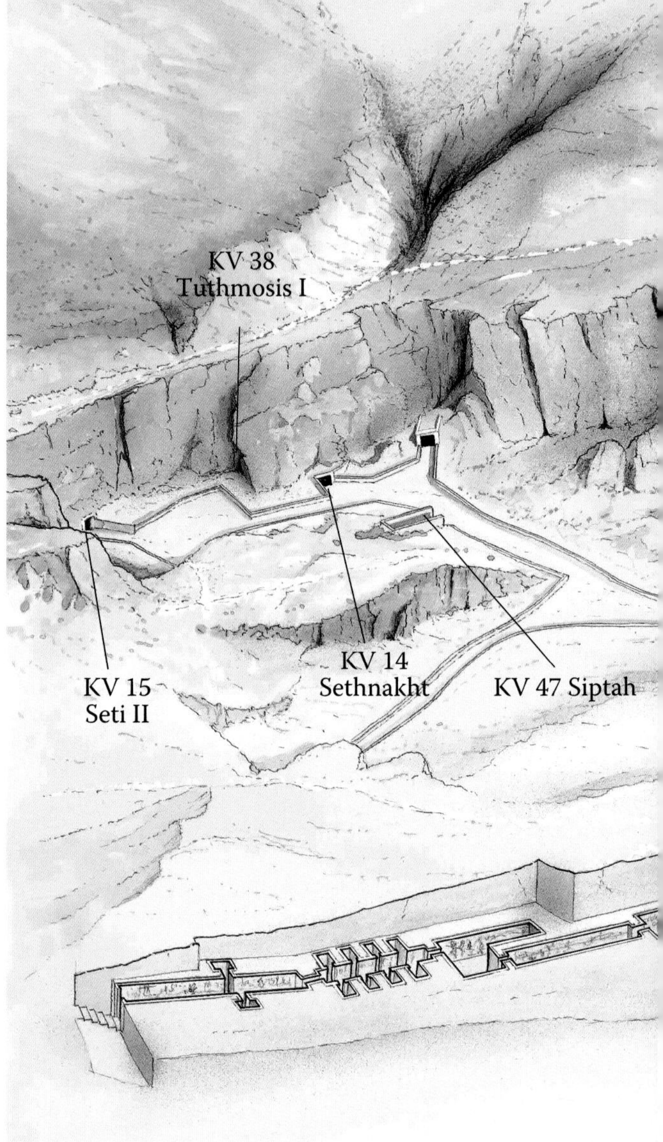

cave in the mountain, each with a name shield around the neck for identification.
Some had been dead for only a few years, and some for many centuries; some had reigned only briefly, some for many decades; some had been the most powerful sovereigns in the entire world. Now, the greatest sovereigns in history lay all together, in no particular order, one beside another. Ahmose, the founder of the 18th Dynasty, lay beside the conqueror Tuthmosis III; the great Ramesses II close by his father Seti I. All in all, the bodies of the pharaohs which were to remain hidden in this anonymous tomb in the heart of the mountain for three thousand years numbered forty.

A young tomb robber named Ahmed Abd el-Rasul, from the village of Qurna, discovered this hiding place by pure chance one day in 1875: for six years he and his brothers succeeded in keeping the secret, and became rich from trade in the objects they gradually stole from the royal mummies.
Then the secret came out and on 5 July 1881, after lengthy questioning, the young Arab led Emil Brugsch, at the time deputy director of the Egyptian Museum of Cairo and brother of the famous Egyptologist, Heinrich, to the entrance of the shaft.
It is hard to imagine what the scholar must have felt when the flickering light of the torches illuminated the

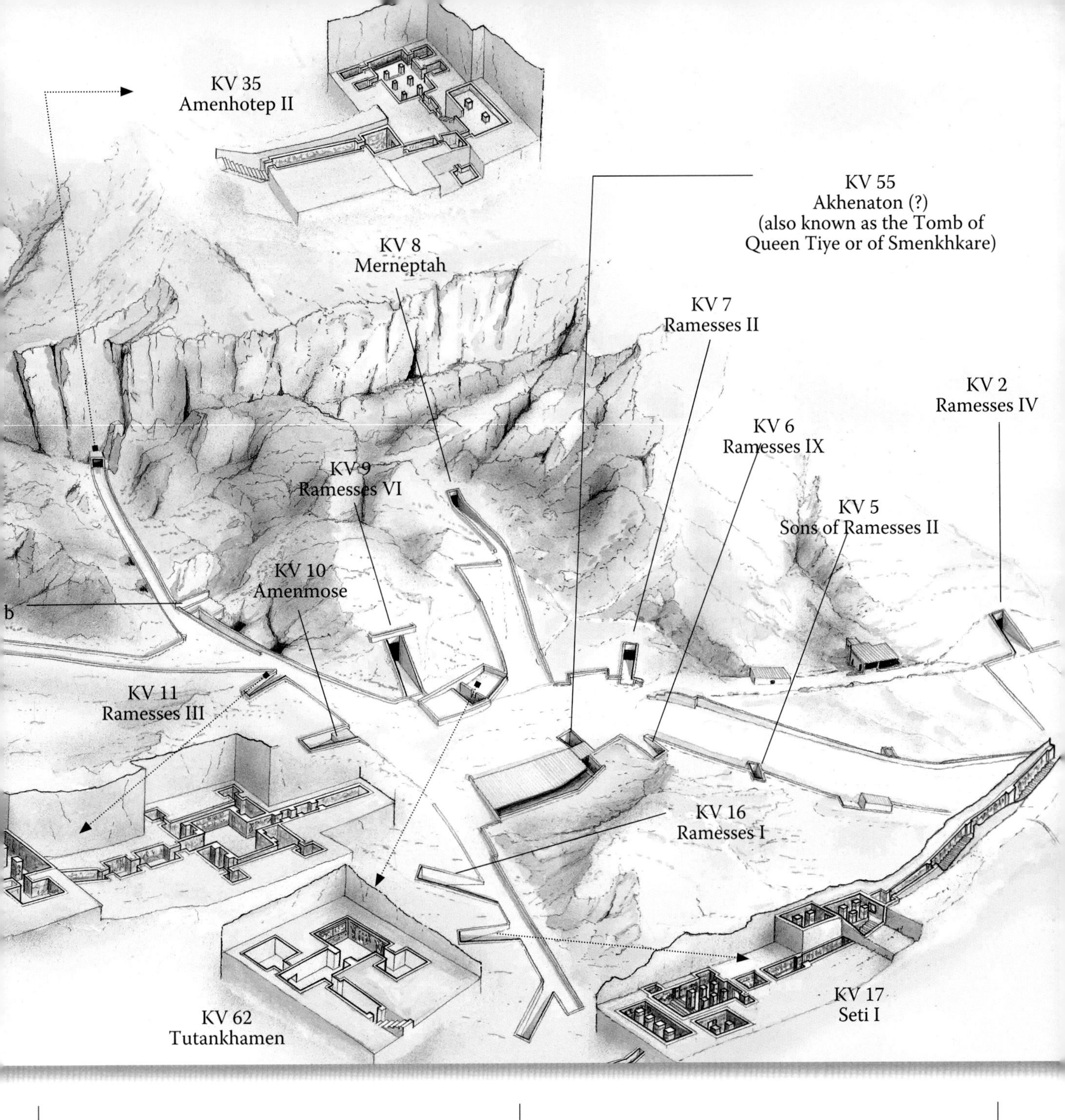

mortal remains of forty sovereigns of the ancient world! A few days later, the mummies were packed and carried down into the valley, where a ship was waiting to take them to Cairo. What happened then was both strange and moving: on hearing that the pharaohs were leaving their centuries-old tomb, the peasants of the valley and their wives crowded along the banks of the Nile, and as the ship slowly passed they rendered homage to their ancient kings, the men firing guns in the air and the women keening laments and scattering dust on their heads and breasts.

The tombs all have more or less the same characteristics: an entrance cut into the rock face, a corridor sloping downwards for about 100 metres with various niches and chambers, the roof supported by pillars, with the sarcophagus chamber at the end. The graffiti on the walls indicate that they have been visited by travellers ever since Greek and Roman times. One of these was the Englishman Dean Stanley, who in 1856 wrote a fine report of his journeys, remarking how seeing the tombs of the Kings was in his opinion tantamount to having seen all of Egyptian religion revealed as it must have been experienced by the most powerful men of Egypt at the most salient moments of their lives.

Tomb of Tutankhamen

The tomb of Tutankhamen consists of a 9 metre-long corridor leading to the antechamber with the funerary chamber and the treasury on the right. From the antechamber the annex is reached, where the offerings and the funerary furnishings were housed. The furnishings are considered to represent one of the greatest treasures of antiquity to have survived intact and they are now housed in the Egyptian Museum in Cairo. In 1922, Lord Carnarvon, an art collector and great traveller, had already invested about £ St 50,000 to finance numerous excavations in Egypt, but all had been unsuccessful. His missions were directed by another Englishman, the archaeologist Howard Carter who had already undertaken excavations in the Valley in 1917, convinced he could find the tomb of Tutankhamen, a pharaoh of transition who brought back the capital to Thebes reviving the ancient cult of Amun-Ra and the other gods, changing his own name from Tutankhatun to Tutankhamen. His was a short-lived reign lasting only nine years and he died aged barely nineteen. Lord Carnarvon had decided that this was to be his last mission in Egypt, but on 4th November 1922, almost at the base of the tomb of Ramesses VI a stone step appeared that led to a second and then a third, descending further until twelve had been cleared, stopping in front of a sealed door, walled in with lime clay. It seemed that this tomb had also been robbed, but to what extent? And most especially, would they find the mummy intact? On the 26th of the same month Carter experienced his greatest day: having broken through a second door bearing intact the seals of the boy pharaoh, he made a small opening with an iron bar and pushed it through the hole, meeting no obstacles. He then tested the air with a candle, not detecting any gases. He finally poked his head through the hole and as his eyes gradually adapted to the darkness, "...strange animals, statues and gold - everywhere the flash of gold, emerged slowly from the darkness...".

A small head in wood and painted plaster found at the entrance to the tomb, portraying Tutankhamen as a child, rising from a lotus bud.

"Marvellous things!" exclaimed Carter, his voice broken with emotion, to Carnarvon who was impatiently asking him what he saw. Of all the precious objects in the sovereign's tomb, the most impressive was the great **sarcophagus**: a single, enormous block of quartzite housed four gilded wooden containers placed one inside the other like Russian dolls; only after 84 days of hard toil dismantling them to bring the 80 pieces composing the four catafalques to light was Carter able to admire the brilliant colours of the paintings decorating the walls of the burial chamber. The sarcophagus was of extraordinary beauty, "worthy of containing the mortal remains of a sovereign". In February 1924, in the presence of a few illustrious guests, a complex winch lifted the ton and a half of granite of the lid. When Carter first shone his light on the interior, he must have been most disappointed: only discoloured linen cloths! But when the linen cloths were slowly cast aside, the king and the gold gradually appeared: a wooden sarcophagus entirely covered in gold leaf and inlaid with glass and semiprecious stones with the pharaoh represented as Osiris, his face expressing great serenity. Almost one year later, on 25th January 1925, Carter tried to open the sarcophagus. The lid of the first anthropoid sarcophagus (2 m. 25 cm. long) was lifted revealing more linen bands and garlands of flowers. By examining the floral wreaths, they were able to establish the season in which the sovereign was buried, between mid-March and late April, because botanists also recognised cornflowers, bittersweet and mandrake, flowers which blossom during that period. Under the sheet they found a second wooden, anthropoid sarcophagus covered with gold leaf and encrusted with cloisonné coloured glass and semi-precious stones. The lid of the second coffin was lifted and even if at this stage Carter had expected to find a third sarcophagus, he certainly did not expect to see in the light of the powerful lamps the amazing sight of the coffin that appeared – a block of solid gold between 2 and 3 ½ mm. thick, weighing more that 110 kilos. "An incredible mass of pure gold": the material itself was priceless! Apart from his head-gear with a cobra and vulture, the king also wears a false beard and a heavy necklace of gold grains and majolica, while holding the whip and sceptre, symbols of the two Egyptian kingdoms. The divinities Nekhbet and Wadjet spread their wings to protect the mummy, while Nephthys and Isis bring the dead pharaoh to life once more. One can just imagine with what awe and suppressed emotion Carter approached the content of this last coffin; he knew that he would have found intact the mummy of

Above, a pectoral in the form of a scarab. The decorative motifs, read from below upwards, form the coronation name of the king, Neb-kheperu-ra.
Left, a detail of a wall in the funerary chamber of the boy pharaoh, representing Tutankhamen in the presence of the goddess Hathor.

Tutankhamen. In fact, the mummy was completely covered in gold and jewels. Here again, the delicate, serene features of the nineteen-year old king appeared on the magnificent **mask** in gold and semiprecious stones that covered the sovereign to his shoulders.
The heavy nemes in blue and gold stripes with the royal symbols on his forehead, inlaid with turquoise lapis lazuli and cornelians, were an impressive sight.
Three sarcophagi, four funeral chapels and many kilos of gold had managed to keep the mortal remains of the great king hidden from the eyes of the world for 132 centuries.

Left, the famous gold mask of Tutankhamen, the most precious item of all the funerary furnishings.

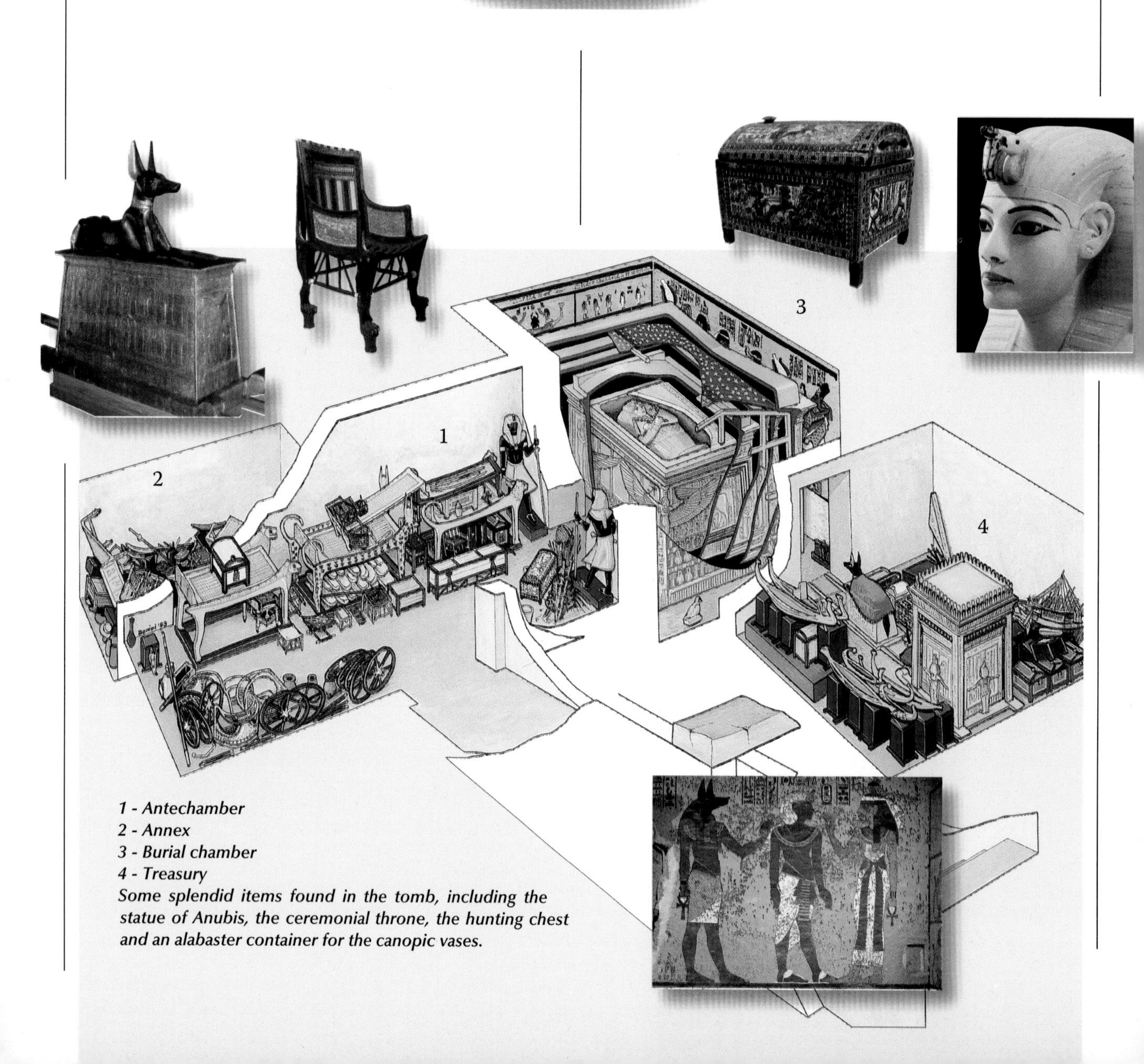

1 - Antechamber
2 - Annex
3 - Burial chamber
4 - Treasury
Some splendid items found in the tomb, including the statue of Anubis, the ceremonial throne, the hunting chest and an alabaster container for the canopic vases.

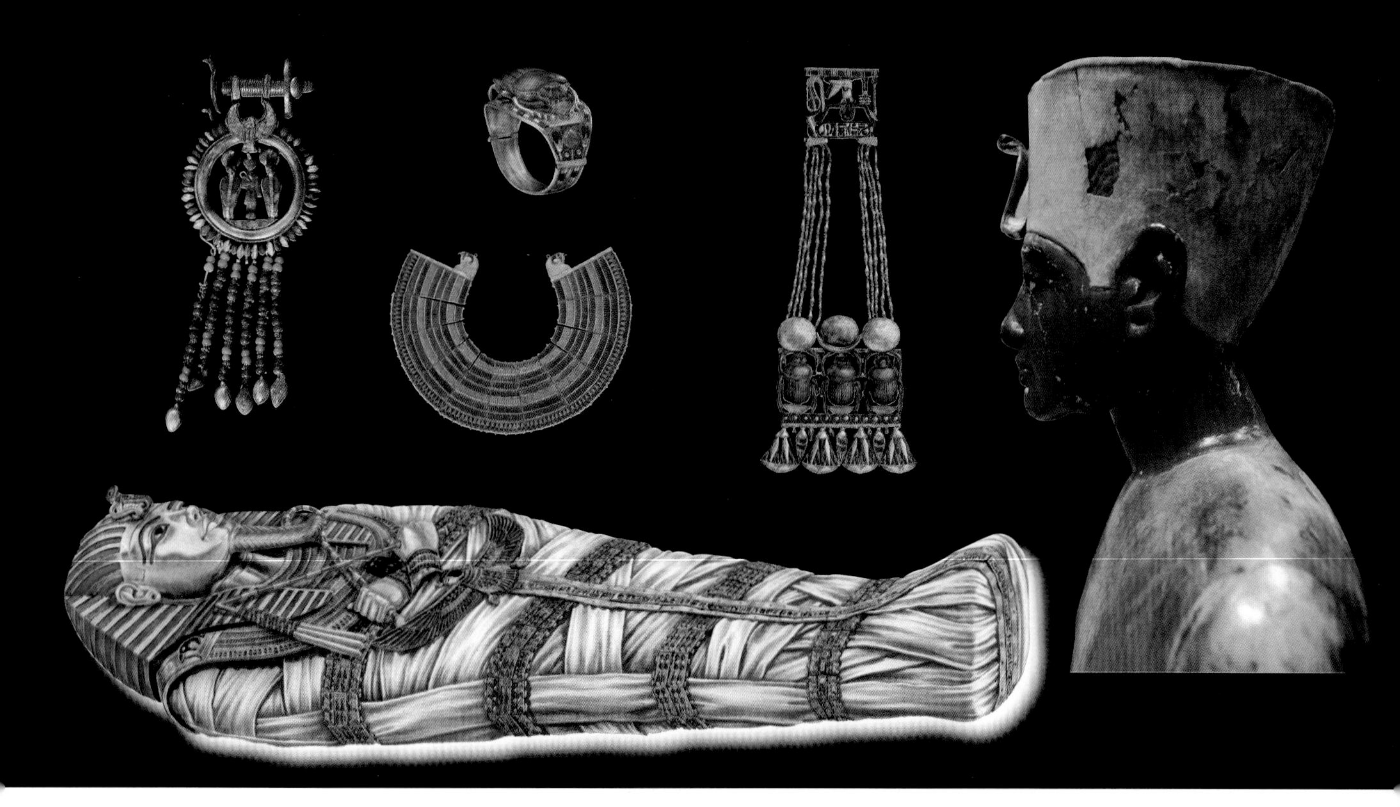

Above, some of the jewels that accompanied the king on his journey to the next world and which Carter found on the mummy: an earring made of lapis lazuli, cornelian, turquoise and green feldspar; gold bracelets with a scarab and floral decorations in yellow quartzite and cornelian; cloissoné necklace the golden clasps of which are in the form of falcons' heads; a smooth gold necklace and pectoral portraying three lapis lazuli scarabs. An elegant bust of the young pharaoh, in plastered and painted wood, with a truncated crown and regal urea.

Below, the funerary chamber with the quartzite sarcophagus that contained the anthropoid sarcophagus inside which the mummy of the pharaoh still lies – the only example of its kind in the Valley of the Kings. Eight metres below the level of the Valley, lying in an east-west direction is the funerary chamber, 6.37 m. wide, 4 m. long, and 3.63 m. high. It is the only room with decorations on the walls, but not the ceiling. The paintings are in the Amarnian style, rather than the usual style found in the Valley, simple and conventional paintings that create a sharp contrast with the yellow plaster which lead to it being named the "House of Gold".

The Tomb of Ramesses III

The tomb is also known as "Bruce's Tomb," from the name of its discoverer, and as the "Harpists' Tomb," after the frescoes which show several men playing the harp in honour of the gods. The pharaoh's sarcophagus, a splendid block of pink granite, was removed from the tomb by the Paduan archaeologist Giovanni Battista Belzoni and later sold to the king of France, who exhibited it in the Louvre. The tomb measures 125 metres in length but lies only 10 metres below the level of the valley. Its present layout was inserted into the earlier tomb of Sethnakhte, Ramesses III's father, whose cartouches are still visible in the first corridor.
Ramesses III was the second sovereign of the 20th Dynasty and was also the last great pharaoh of the New Kingdom. A confusing period of internecine wars and disorders followed his reign, and Egypt precipitated into chaos. Ramesses III initiated important administrative and social reforms. In the eighth year of his reign, he inflicted a heavy defeat on a coalition of the "Sea Peoples" and Libyan tribes; the great battle on the Delta is illustrated in the relief sculptures on the walls of the Temple of Medinet Habu, where Peleset prisoners, who later settled in Palestine and called themselves Philistines, are shown. In the 29th year of his reign, Ramesses III fell victim to a palace conspiracy, as we learn from a scroll known as the *Judicial Papyrus*, now in the Egyptian Museum of Turin, that documents the capture and judging of the guilty parties.

Some examples of the paintings in the tomb of Ramesses III, portraying two Syrians identified by the pointed beard and the presence of a band in their hair.
Below right, the pharaoh Ramesses III is represented making an offering to the gods.

The Tomb of Ramesses IV

The first tomb along the approach to the centre of the Valley is small (66 metres long), and contains the sarcophagus of Ramesses IV, sovereign of the 20th Dynasty and son of Ramesses III. The plan of the tomb appears on a papyrus in the Egyptian Museum of Turin. As early as the 5th century, it was used as a church by a small Christian community in the Valley. The plan of the tomb appears on a papyrus in the Egyptian Museum of Turin. The splendid decorations of the tomb are predominately texts, with scenes from the *Book of the Dead*, the *Book of the Gates*, and the *Book of the Caverns*.

The sarcophagus of the pharaoh inside the funerary chamber: measuring 3.30 m. in length and 2.74 in height, it is the largest in the entire Valley. On the lid is a relief of Ramesses IV between the goddesses Isis and Nephthys.

The Tomb of Ramesses IX

This unfortunately quite damaged tomb belongs to one of the last Ramessides of the 20th Dynasty, whose reign was marked by a long series of domestic disorders and by famine.
When it was opened, the tomb was found to contain an enormous pair of skids from the sledge on which the pharaoh's sacred boat was transported. Another interesting find consisted of several hundred shards on which the tomb labourers had recorded the number of tools, the hours of work, the list of provisions, and so on. The tomb consists of a long staircase leading to a corridor that opens onto two rooms, one of which has four pillars, and a second smaller corridor that ends at the sarcophagus chamber.

Some scenes from the decoration of the tomb of Ramesses IX: above, the pharaoh is represented once with the crown of Upper Egypt and once with the crown of Lower Egypt. Left, the boat of the sun god, Ra with a ram's head; standing in front of him are the goddess Nebet-Uia, the gods Seth and Wepwawet and benign serpents. Below, a symbolic scene with the sacred scarab and the sun king, Ra.

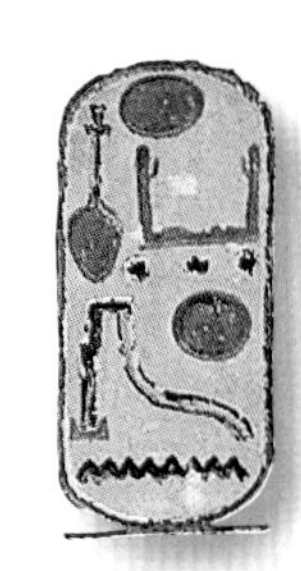

The Tomb of Ramesses VI

Known in antiquity as the Tomb of Memnon and also as La Tombe de la Métempsychose (Napoleonic expedition, 1798), the tomb of Ramesses VI was discovered by James Burton, an Englishman. Like the other great Ramesside tombs, its entrance is set high, about 400 metres above the valley floor, exactly the contrary of the deeply-dug shaft tombs of the 18th Dynasty.

The front part is the oldest and was begun at the time of Ramesses V. It was later enlarged and is quite linear in form, with a corridor leading to an antechamber, a pillared hall, a second corridor, and a second antechamber which precedes the burial chamber, where the ceiling is entirely decorated with astronomical scenes and the creation of the sun. A gigantic sky goddess, Nut, portrayed twice, enfolds the western sphere. The tomb, in which many remains of workers' tools were found, was known and visited from oldest times as is evident from the many Greek and Coptic graffiti on the walls.

Above right and right, details of the decoration on the ceiling of the burial chamber, with the goddess Nut and the heavenly gods. Above, the god Thoth represented on a pillar with the head of an Ibis and the crescent moon. Centre, the sarcophagus chamber, painted by Hector Horeau.

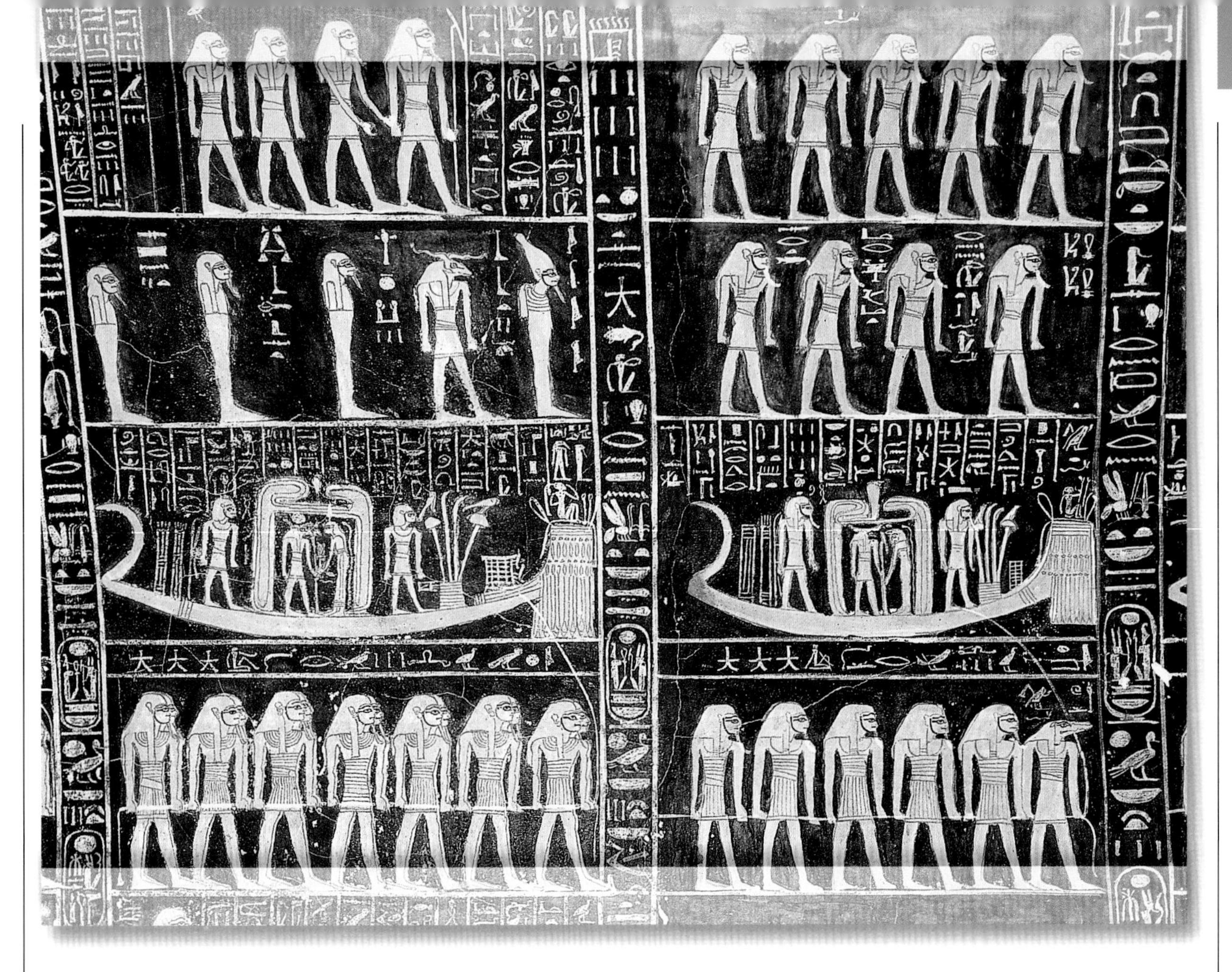

Another detail of the ceiling in the tomb of Ramesses VI, with scenes from the Book of the Day and the Book of the Night.

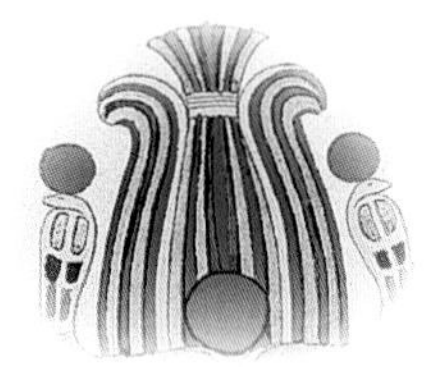

Tomb of Merneptah

The plan of the tomb is very simple, a long corridor in sections descending to the room that still contains the sarcophagus. The scenes illustrated there are the traditional funeral myth scenes.
Merneptah, fourth and last pharaoh of the 19th Dynasty, thirteenth son of Ramesses II and Isinofret is buried here. He was already elderly when he came to power and while his father was considered the pharaoh of the Jewish slavery in Egypt, Merneptah himself was considered the pharaoh of the Exodus. In fact, under him the name of Israel appeared for the first time in a granite stele: "Desolated Israel, that has lost its seed, Palestine is a widow under Egypt". The mummy of Merneptah was not found in this tomb but in the tomb of Amenhotep II. He was responsible for the military campaign against the "sea peoples": the ancient Libyans and their allies, the Lukka, Aqiyawasa, Saradn and Tarusa, recognizable today as the Lycians, the Achaeans, the Sards and Etruscans.

Below, the pharaoh Merneptah portrayed with the double plumed crown and horns of a ram. He is standing before the god Horus, with the head of a falcon.

The Tomb of Horemheb

Horemheb, the last pharaoh of the 18th Dynasty, was not of royal blood; from a family of governors, he had been chief of archers under Amenhotep IV, of whom he was a great friend. Having risen to the rank of general, he succeeded the elderly Ay on the throne, denied the ancient Atonian religion and cancelled the name of Tutankhamen, the earlier predecessor, replacing it with his own. Among his most brilliant undertakings was the peace stipulated with the Hittite king Mursilis II. Until this discovery, it was generally thought that Horemheb's tomb was in the desert near Memphis.
The English archaeologist Edward Ayrton found the name of the general-pharaoh, in hieratic script, on a tablet regarding inspections of the royal tombs in the Valley. The tomb represents a transition from the simpler tombs of the 18th Dynasty to the more elaborate ones that would appear later. In fact, the corridor no longer takes a sharp right-angle but, after a slight initial curve, proceeds in a practi-

Left, three examples of hieroglyph writing painted on the walls of Horemheb's tomb: a duck, a buzzard and a falcon are identifiable. Right, Amunet, a funerary goddess of the west. Below left, Ptah, god of the shadow world represented as a mummy with the calotte on his head. Below right, Horemheb offers two round jars to the gods.

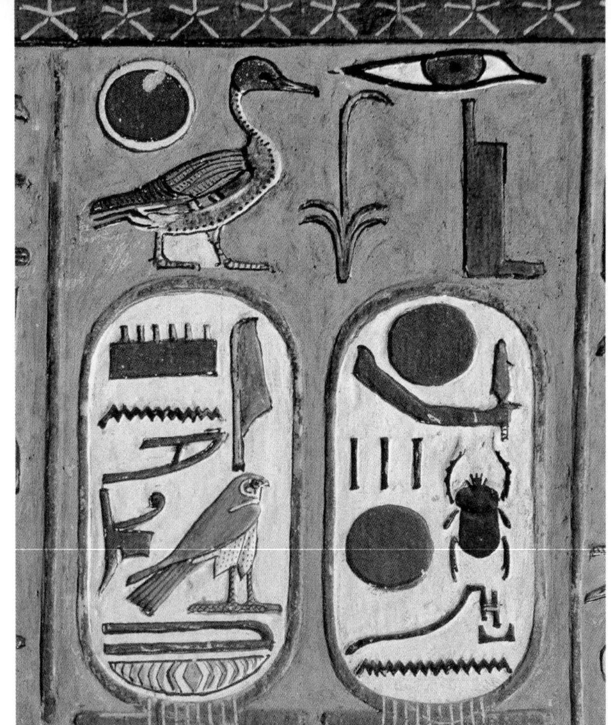

cally straight line to the burial chamber. On discovery, the archaeologists found the bas-reliefs depicting the usual funeral repertory to be as brilliantly coloured and as perfect, fresh, and luminous as if they had just been painted.

Above, the goddess Hathor with the horns of a cow and solar disc, and the bright colours of the cartouche with the hieroglyphs of Horemheb's name, "Meryamun Djeser-kheperu-ra Setep-en-ra".

Below, the quartzite sarcophagus which contained the mummy of Amenhotep II.

AMENHOTEP II, THE ATHLETE-PHARAOH

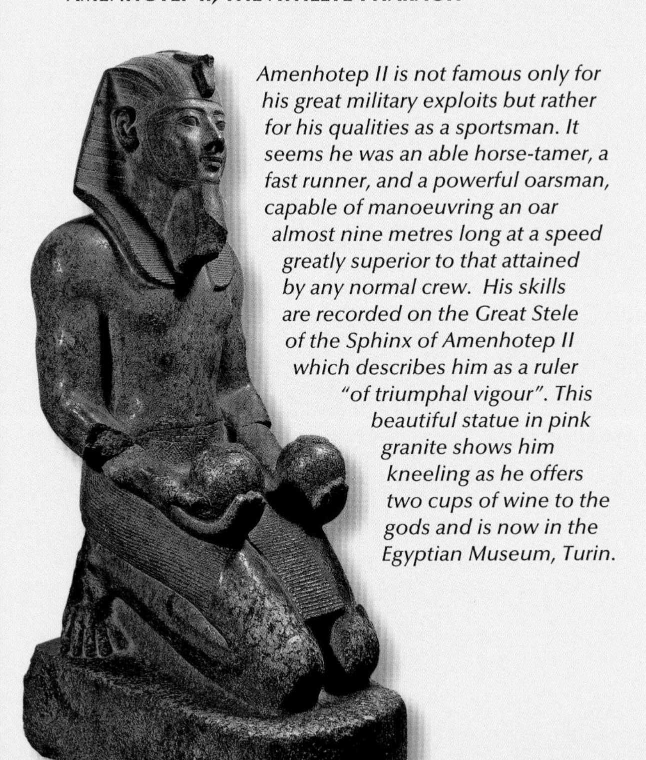

Amenhotep II is not famous only for his great military exploits but rather for his qualities as a sportsman. It seems he was an able horse-tamer, a fast runner, and a powerful oarsman, capable of manoeuvring an oar almost nine metres long at a speed greatly superior to that attained by any normal crew. His skills are recorded on the Great Stele of the Sphinx of Amenhotep II which describes him as a ruler "of triumphal vigour". This beautiful statue in pink granite shows him kneeling as he offers two cups of wine to the gods and is now in the Egyptian Museum, Turin.

The Tomb of Amenhotep II

Son of Tuthmosis III, Amenhotep II ruled Egypt from 1450 to 1425 BC. He oppressed a Syrian revolt and had his son and successor, Tuthmosis IV, marry Mutemuya, daughter of the Mitannian king. The burial chamber contains the great quartzite *sarcophagus*, which, when it was discovered, still contained the pharaoh's mummy, with a garland of mimosa flowers encircling the neck. The mummy was displayed in the tomb until 1934, when it was transported to Cairo Museum.

The Tomb of Ramesses I

The founder of the 19th Dynasty was a regular army officer, a general, and the vizier of Horemheb whom he succeeded in 1314 BC. His reign was very brief, barely two years, but in this period - as witnessed by the bas-reliefs in the hypostyle hall of Karnak - he advanced into Hittite territory "as far as the land of Kadesh." He immediately took his son Seti I as coregent and chose Tanis as capital of the empire.

The structure of his tomb, discovered by Belzoni, is rather spare, since evidently the elderly pharaoh died suddenly while work was still in progress.

Above, scenes from the Book of the Doors; left, Ramesses I between Horus and Anubis with the scrolls of his titles; below, the serpent Apophis, symbol of evil, and the wall with the solar boat of Ra and the struggle of Atum against Apophis; on the wall beside, Ramesses I makes an offering to the god Nefertum.

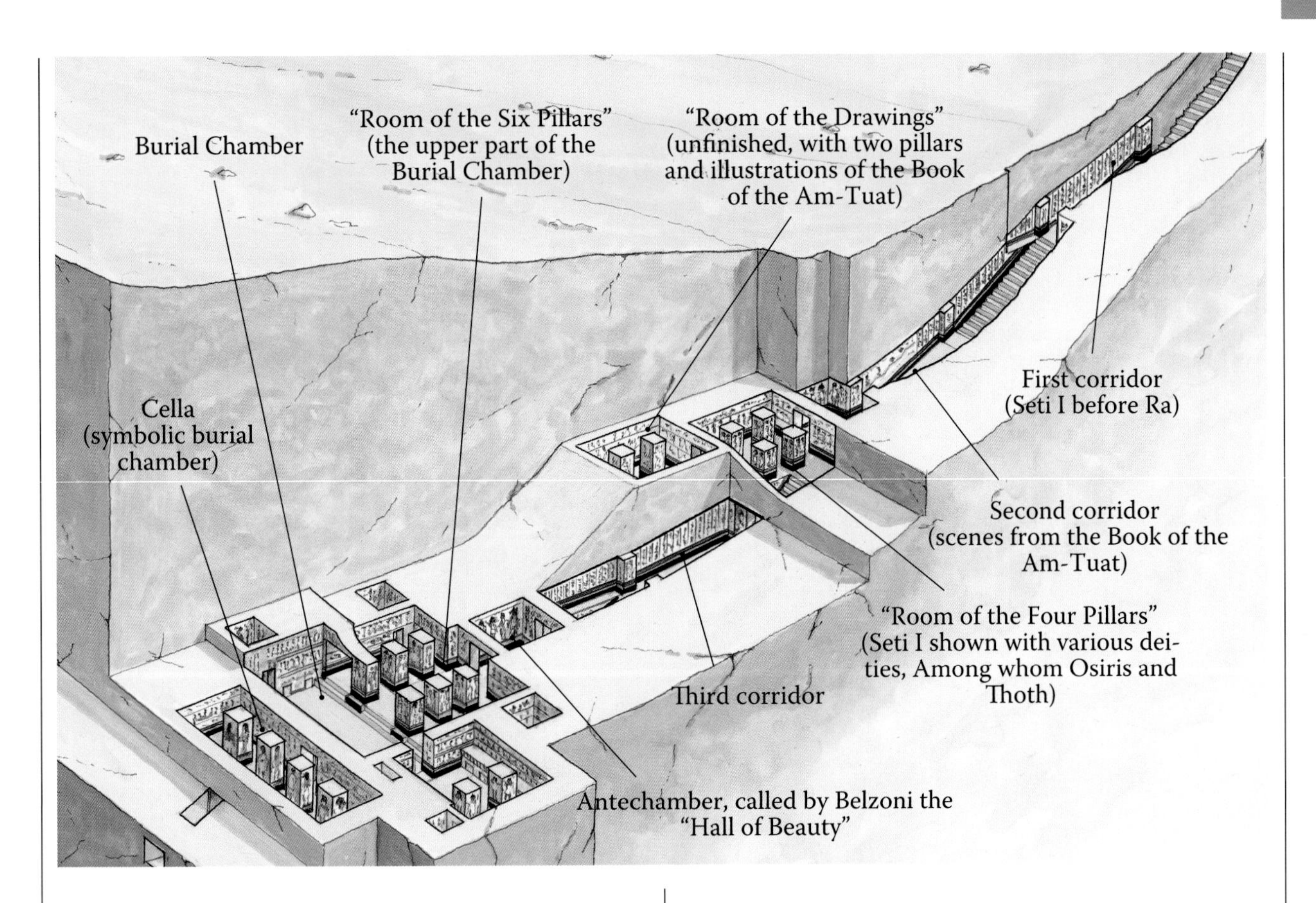

The Tomb of Seti I

The tomb of Seti I is one of the most spectacular in the Valley of the Kings, and the pharaoh who was buried there was also one of the most important of his dynasty, the 19th. Son of Ramesses I, he was chief archer and vizier while his father lived. As pharaoh, Seti I continued the policy of expansion into the East: he advanced into Syria as far as Tyre, drove back the advance of the Hittite chief Muwatallis, and recaptured Phoenicia. The tomb, discovered in October of 1817 by Belzoni and known at length by the archaeologist's name alone, is 105 metres long; 27 steep steps descend immediately to a much lower level. Here, a corridor leads to a second

Following page: Seti I engraved on a pilaster in the first room; below, scenes from the Book of the Dead, with the serpent protecting the boat, and Ra with a ram's head.

An image of the gods on the lake of fire.

flight of steps leading to a second corridor ending in a room in which Belzoni found a shaft, evidently dug to confuse unwanted visitors.
Belzoni noted a crack of 65 centimetres on the opposite wall; after daringly crossing the shaft, he widened the opening and discovered that it led to rooms the original builders had hoped to keep hidden.
Even so, none of these contained the sarcophagus - Belzoni was, in fact, only halfway there. More corridors, more staircases, and more rooms finally led him to the sarcophagus chamber - but not the mummy, which was discovered only seventy years later, in Deir el-Bahri, while the lovely sarcophagus is today part of the Soane Collection in London. Apparently, however, the tomb was supposed to go even deeper into the heart of the earth. Belzoni began exploring a mysterious gallery that starts under the sarcophagus, but after about ninety metres the lack of air and the friability of the rock forced him to stop. A further thirty metres were dug during the 1950s. This gallery however, has remained a mystery and we still have not found out what purpose it served and where it led. But ancient legend in the Valley has it that the tunnel crosses the entire mountain before it comes out in the open near the temple of Hatshepsut in Deir el-Bahri.
Belzoni maintained that this was the finest tomb ever discovered in Egypt; the walls, columns, and ceilings are in fact literally covered with painted and bas-relief decoration full of meaning and symbolism.

One of the outstanding elements in the magnificent decoration of the tomb of Seti I is the image of Osiris between two fetishes that symbolise rebirth. Above, the wall separating the kingdom of Duat from that of Osiris, with doors protected by guardians. Below, a detail of the decoration showing the procession of sacred boats, including the boat carrying Ra with the ram's head.

The Tomb of Tuthmosis III

The tomb of Tuthmosis III, one of the greatest pharaohs of Egypt, was discovered in 1898 by Victor Loret who succeeded Gaston Maspero as director of the Egyptian Antiquities Service. The entrance to the tomb was concealed in a rocky crevice about 10 metres above the floor of the valley. It consisted of two corridors with two steep flights of steps leading to a ritual shaft that ended in a vestibule with two supporting pillars. The funerary chamber was oval in shape, as was the massive red quartzite sarcophagus which was situated on the east side of the room. When it was discovered, the lid lay broken on the floor. The most important feature of this tomb is the decoration illustrating scenes of the journey of the sun in the world of the dead, in a highly graphic, almost surreal style.

Rightly known as the "Napoleon of Antiquity", Tuthmosis III was the illegitimate son of Tuthmosis II and, on the death of his father, became pharaoh at a very early age. He was deposed, however, by his aunt and step-mother, Hatshepsut, wife of the deceased pharaoh, who proclaimed herself regent and for twenty five years forced him to remain in exile. Tuthmosis III only succeeded in regaining the throne on the death of his aunt, and indulged in his own belated vendetta by erasing the name, the cartouches, and the images of the hated queen from all the monuments in Egypt, replacing it with his own and his father's names. Under his rule the country enjoyed one of its most glorious moments: his seventeen military campaigns in Syria demonstrated a great understanding of strategy and profound knowledge of military tactics. Egypt reached the height of its power and his victories have remained famous: Kadesh, Megiddo, (where he defeated 330 Syrian princes), Karkhemish. When Tuthmosis III died, he was about 70 years old and the country he left was rich and strong, extending from the river Euphrates to the fourth cataract of the Nile in Sudan.

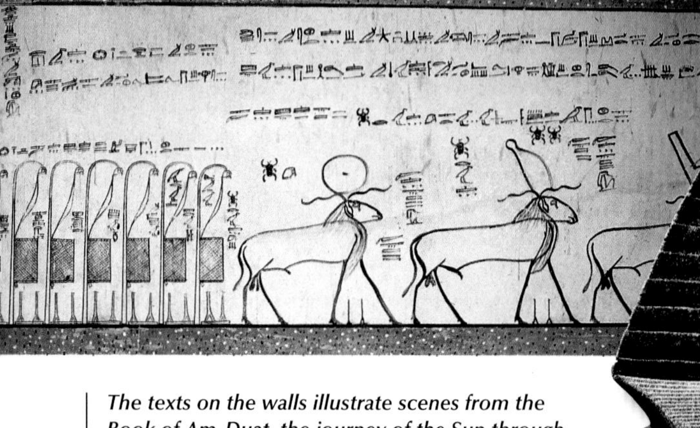

The texts on the walls illustrate scenes from the Book of Am-Duat, the journey of the Sun through the Afterworld.

The pharaoh Tuthmosis III represented in a black granite statue from Karnak, now exhibited in the Egyptian Museum in Cairo.

In the vestibule to the tomb of Tuthmosis III is a complete list of all the divinities of the Duat, with the goddesses praising Ra and the cynocephalous gods opening the doors to the great god.

The Valley of the Queens

The Valley of the Queens, also known as *Biban el-Harim*, begins about 1.5 kilometres south west of the Valley of the Kings. The ancient Egyptians gave it the evocative name of Set Neferu, meaning "a place of beauty". Princesses and princes from the royal houses of the 19th to the 20th Dynasties are buried here. The tombs (about 110 have been identified) were either simple funerary shafts without any decoration, or were entire architectural structures enhanced with beautiful wall paintings.
The tomb of Nefertari, the most beautiful of all the Theban tombs, was discovered by Ernesto Schiaparelli who lead the Italian archaeological expedition between 1903 and 1906.

A view of the entrance to the Valley of the Queens and below, a painting from the tomb of Amen-hir-Khopshef showing Ramesses III in front of the god Ptah of Memphis.

Above, the goddess Neith of Sais and, on the right, Horus dressed in a leopard skin, portrayed on the first pilaster in the sarcophagus room.

The Tomb of Nefertari

This tomb, discovered in 1904 by the Italian Archaeological Expedition lead by Ernesto Schiaparelli, was dug into the west flank of the valley for Nefertari, Meri-en-Mut, wife of Ramesses II and without doubt the best-loved of the many wives of this great pharaoh, who built the architectural jewel of the Small Temple at Abu Simbel for her. The tomb is 27.5 metres long and lies about eight metres below ground level: since the layer of rock into which it is dug is particularly fragile, the walls were bonded with such a thick layer of plaster that their pictorial decoration seems to be in relief. When the tomb was discovered, it was immediately apparent that it had been violated from early times: all the tomb furnishings had disappeared and the mummy of the woman who had been one of the most famous queens of Egypt was reduced to a few sad remains. Only the splendid paintings survived to bear witness to the fact that this tomb had in its time been the most important and loveliest of the entire Valley of the Queens. In 1986, an agreement between the Egyptian Antiquities Service and the Getty Conservation Institute launched a project for systematic recovery of the painted decoration of the tomb. Restoration work began in 1988 and was concluded in April 1992.

Returned to their original splendour, these paintings are further evidence of how complex and deeply-rooted were the spiritual and religious beliefs of the New Kingdom.

The goddess Wadjet represented as a serpent with the red crown; Anubis in the form of a jackal with the flail and red band; below, Isis and Nephthys beside Ra with a ram's head and red disc supported by the horns; a detail of the goddess Selket.

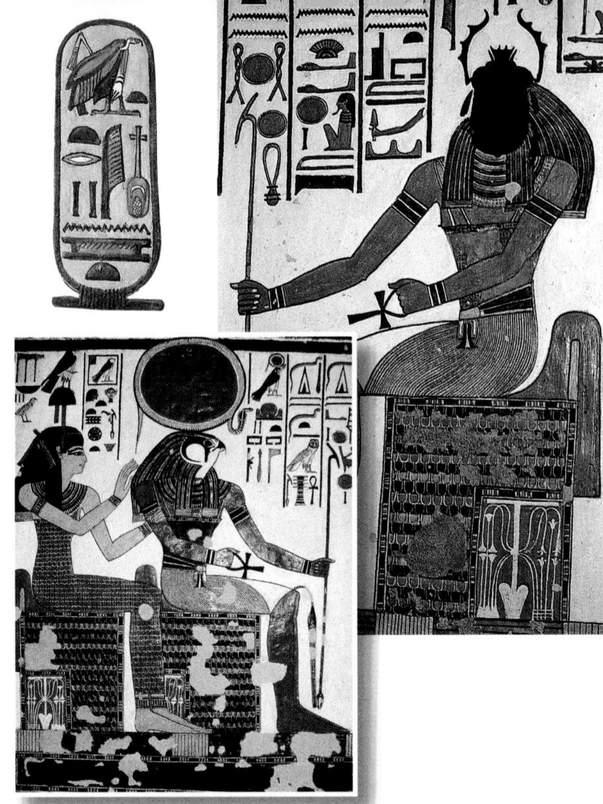

Left, Osiris wearing the two plumed crown, while holding in his hands the sceptre of power and the flail. Above, the cartouche of the queen, the god Khephri, and Hathor and Ra-Harakhti seated. Facing page, the splendid decorations on the pilasters of the sarcophagus rooms.

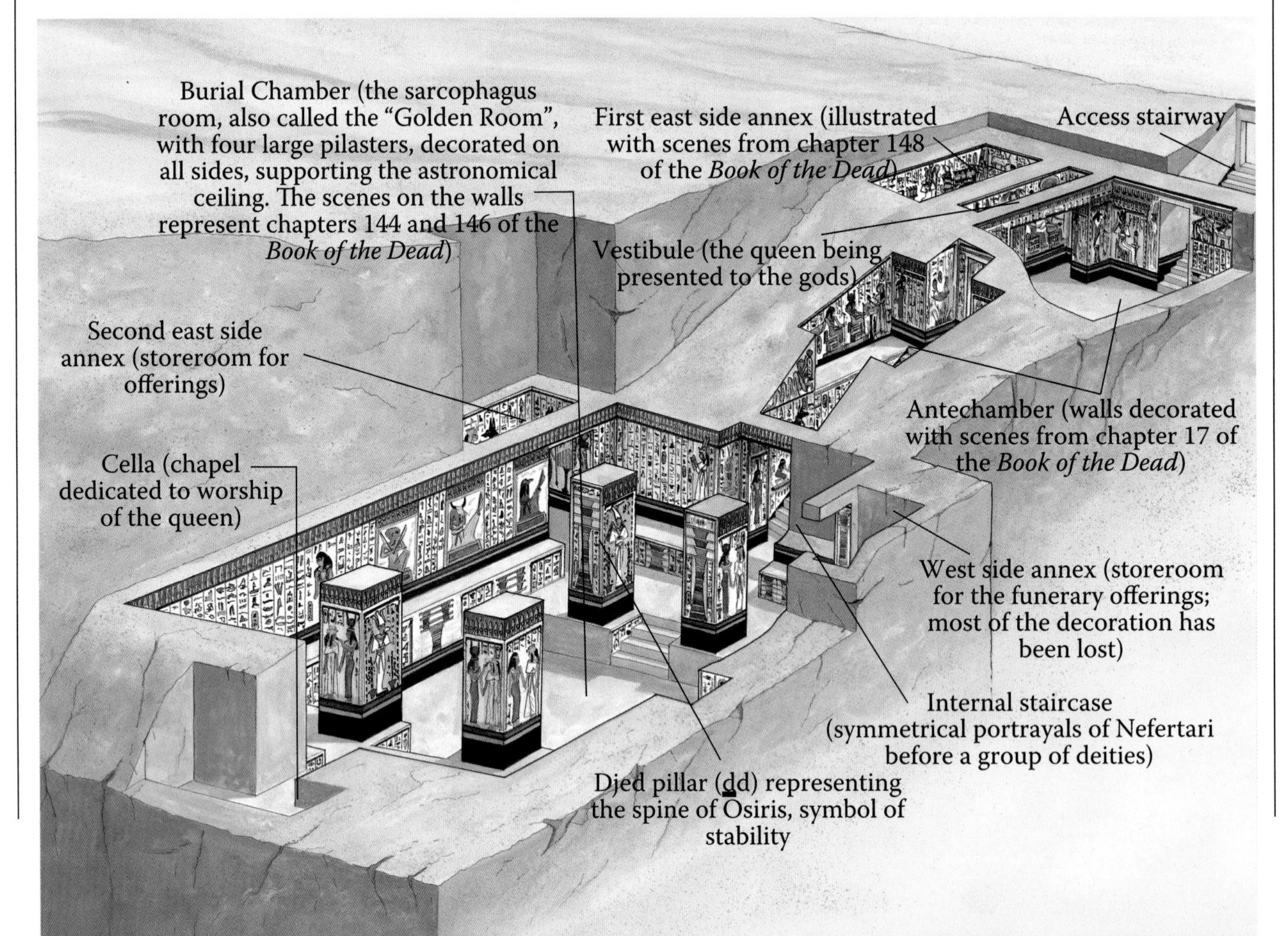

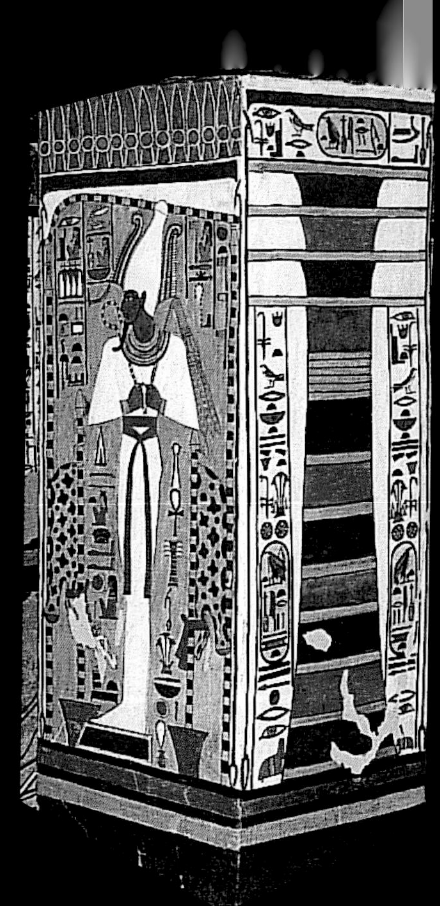

The Tomb of Amen-Hir-Khopshef

This tomb was originally built to contain the remains of another prince and son of Ramesses III, and only later became that of Amen-hir-Khopshef. Extremely simple in structure - a staircase leads to a square room and a corridor, which in turn leads to the *burial chamber* - the tomb is characterized by decoration in lively, intense colours; an unusual shade of turquoise predominates throughout.

Above, Ramesses III, embraced by the goddess Isis and prince Amen-hir-Khopshef, shown with a shaved head and a plait tied on one side only, a style worn by all young Egyptian males. Left, a beautiful, brilliantly coloured detail of the falcon god, Horus.

The Tomb of Queen Tyti

Tyti was the wife of one of the numerous Rameses of the 20th Dynasty, perhaps Rameses IV. Her long-abandoned tomb, which had even been used as a stable for donkeys, is, however, in quite good condition and is distinguished by its interesting limestone *relief decoration* dominated by a light pink colour.

A wall in the tomb of Tyti and the goddess Hathor represented as a cow.

The Tomb of Prince Para'Hirwenemef

Para'Hirwenemef was another of the sons of Ramesses III. The predominant colours are ochre yellow and pink. The wall decoration of this tomb mainly represents the deceased prince being presented to the various gods by the pharaoh.

Left, two seated baboons and one standing, armed with a long knife.
Above, three more guardians watching over the doors of the Duat Underworld; one is seen facing us, one has the head of a crocodile and another the head of a vulture.

Tomb of Kha'emweset

Prince Kha'emweset, another son of Ramesses III and probably the younger brother of Amen-hir-Khopshef, was given a tomb that is similar to those of the kings in its ground plan, even though, naturally, it is much smaller. As in the tombs of other princes, the decoration is quite lively, with scenes of offerings and tributes in intense, brilliant colours. When the tomb was discovered in 1903, the corridor was almost completely blocked by sarcophagi - and in fact the tomb had been reused on numerous occasions.

Of all the beautiful decorations in this tomb, the portrayal of the genie Hery-maat is outstanding, represented here as a naked young man with the khayt headdress.
The other subjects alternate hieroglyphic symbols with images of various deities.

Deir el-Bahri

The Temple of Hatshepsut

One thousand two hundred years after Imhotep, another architect, Senmut, appeared on the scene of Egyptian history and created another architectural masterpiece. Queen Hatshepsut, a patron of the arts and a military leader, ordered a funerary monument for her father Tuthmosis I and for herself and chose an isolated valley already dedicated to the goddess Hathor who, in the form of a heifer, received the deceased in the Afterworld. Queen Hatshepsut's monument was in later times abandoned; at one point in history it became a Christian convent called the Convent of the North, and this fact not only protected the pharaonic temple from further destruction but also gave the area its present name of Deir el-Bahri. The famous architect and minister, Senmut, brilliantly exploited the dramatic fan of ochre-coloured rock that stretches out behind the monument, which was built according to a new and revolutionary concept. The east-facing Temple of Hatshepsut, called in antiquity Djeser-djeseru, "more splendid than splendid," is unique in Egyptian architecture. It consisted of a series of vast terraces which, via ramps, led up to the sanctuary. An avenue of sphinxes and obelisks led up to the first terrace, closed at the back by a portico of 22 pillars and flanked by two Osiris pillars, from which another ramp led to the second terrace, also equipped with a portico of two rows of square pillars. On one of the walls, beautiful bas-reliefs narrate the stories of the queen's birth and childhood and of the expedition sent by her to the mysterious land of Punt, most probably today's Somalia, to judge from the giraffes, monkeys, panther skins, and ivory objects that are shown. On the last wall, 18 niches, large and small, must have held just as many statues of the queen in standing

Detail of an Osiris pilaster representing Hatshepsut with a beard, traditionally an attribute of male royal dignitaries.
Below, a view of the monumental complex of Deir el-Bahri and, on the right, the elegant columns with Hathor capitals.

and seated poses. Also located in the temple is the 16-faceted pillar so admired for its elegance by Champollion that he called it "proto-Doric."

The entire left side of the valley was occupied by the gigantic **mortuary Temple of Montuhotep I** built five hundred years before Hatshepsut decided to install hers in the same place. In the main, the tomb reflects the architectural canons typical of the Old Kingdom, but in many respects also heralds New Kingdom tomb structure. The monumental complex of Montuhotep consists of a gigantic *tomb* with a *pyramidal tumulus*, at the centre of which was the king's sepulchre.

A view of the temple clearly showing the column with sixteen facets, also known as proto-Doric and very similar to the later Greek column. The column and pilaster with the head of the goddess with cow's ears, surmounted by a sistrum were known as Hathor or sistrum columns.

On the left of the third courtyard is the chapel of Hathor and on the right, the chapel of Anubis. Both are decorated with lively colours.

Medinet Habu

For a long time, Medinet Habu was considered nothing more than a rich quarry where large ready-dressed stones could be found. In Christian times, a village rose and occupied most of the temple area - which the Copts called the *Mound of Djeme* - and, for once, this new use actually helped to preserve many remains which otherwise would have been lost.

The monumental complex of Medinet Habu includes the *Temple of Ramesses III*, preceded by the *shrine of Tuthmosis I* and the *chapels* of the adoring divinities of Amun. Formidable, almost military in appearance, is the fine *Southern Gate*, also known as the "Royal Pavilion", the form of which was inspired by Syrian fortified cities called *migdal*. Set between two towers, above this triumphal gate are two rows of longitudinal windows. The martial aspect of this construction is further emphasized by the bas-reliefs on the walls of the towers: exemplary massacres of prisoners, the pharaoh leading captured enemies to the god Amun, and so on. Through further pylons and three hypostyle halls, the central sanctuary is reached where two groups of statues stand, one representing Ramesses III with the god Thoth and the other, the pharaoh with Ma'at.

Facing page, the Door of the South, or Royal Pavilion, and the first courtyard of Ramesses III's temple. This page, two statues of Sekhmet, the lioness deity; an architrave of the temple with the goddess Nekhbet portrayed as a vulture; the Osiris pilasters that flank the right side of the first courtyard of Ramesses III's temple.

The Ramesseum

Ramesseum is the name given in the 19th century to the funerary temple that Ramesses II had built on the west bank of the Nile between the desert and the village now called Qurna. His "temple of millions of years" was built by the architect Penreh on such a large scale that it was greater than all others of the time, as was recorded by the historian Diodorus Siculus. Ramesses II did not hesitate to remove stone and decorative elements from the Temples of Hatshepsut at Deir el-Bahri for its construction. Today, sadly, only a few fascinating ruins remain: the Osiris pillars on the façade of the *hypostyle hall* and, like a toppled giant, the badly damaged statue of the seated Ramesses II enthroned, which it is calculated must have been 17 metres tall and weighed more than 1,000 tons. Diodorus Siculus incorrectly interpreted the coronation name of the Pharaoh as User-Maat-Ra, and recorded that the statue represented Ozymandias.

Facing page, the temple of Medinet Habu: a pair of statues representing Ramesses III and the god Thoth.

This page, images of the Ramesseum: a view of the temple and the head of the lost colossus of Ramesses II.

A pilaster decorated with the figure of the pharaoh and two images of the Ramesseum showing the Osiris pilasters in the atrium on the façade of the hypostyle hall. Only the columns in the central rows and part of the ceiling decorated with gold stars on a blue background still exist.

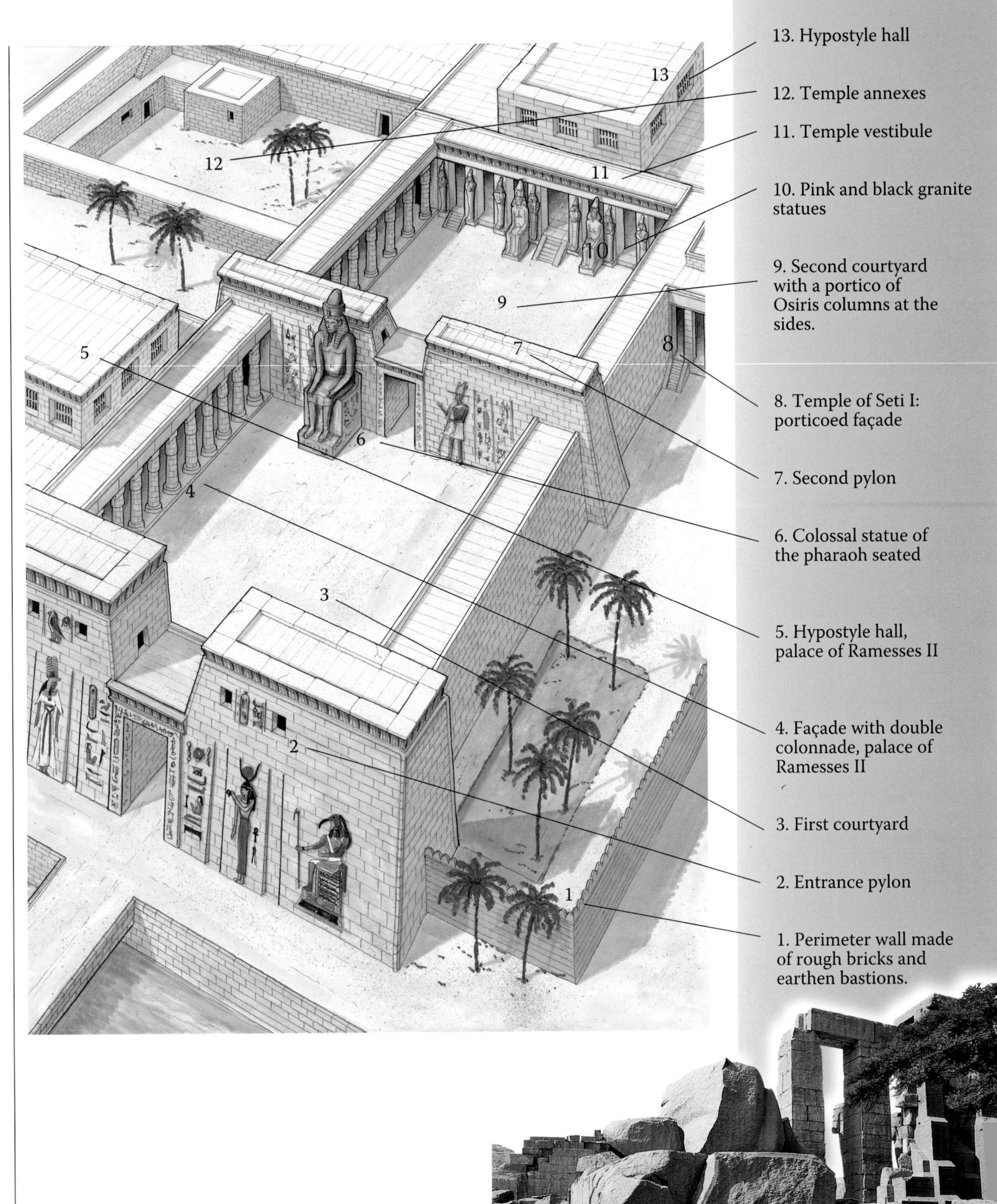

Today sadly only fragments of the colossus of Ramesses II remain, yet they show that despite the size, there was a great attention to detail. The toe nail alone measured 19 cm.

The Valley of the Nobles

In the three neighbouring areas of Assassif, Khokhah and Sheik Abd el-Qurna, impressive necropoli are located with dignitaries of the dynasties of the Middle Kingdom. Compared with the tombs of the pharaohs, those of the high dignitaries of the Middle Kingdom dynasties are architecturally extremely simple and all have the same layout. They are preceded by an open-air terrace, followed by a vestibule with painted walls illustrating the terrestrial occupations of the owner.

A corridor leads to a niche where a statue of the deceased, sometimes together with those of his wife or relatives, is often found. The paintings in these tombs are characterized by freshness and vivacity and an unusual realism, and bear witness to life at court in ancient Egypt. The most frequent subjects are funeral banquets with music and dancing, work in the fields, crafts activities, and scenes of daily life in general.

An image of Sennufer, who is buried in the tomb, with his wife Senetnefer.

The Tomb of Sennufer

A flight of 43 steps cut into the rock takes us into the lovely tomb of Sennufer, prince of the Southern City (Thebes) and Superintendent of the Granaries and Livestock of Amun under Amenhotep II.
The anonymous painter of this tomb decorated the ceiling with a marvellous pergola of purple grapes.

The daughter of the deceased is also represented in the tomb – the young Mutahi is portrayed in miniature at the feet of her father during a banquet.

The Tomb of Rekhmire

This tomb, which structurally could be taken as an example of a Theban civilian tomb during the 18th Dynasty, belonged to Rekhmire, Viceroy and Governor of Thebes and vizier under Amenhotep III and Akhenaton. Both the vestibule and the chapel are decorated and the paintings are of immense historical interest since they provide many invaluable illustrations, in a great number of scenes, of Egypt's relations with other countries at the time. The liveliest depictions are those in which representatives of foreign countries bring their offerings: the emissaries of the land of Punt (probably Somalia), carrying ebony, ivory, and ostrich feathers, are clearly identifiable; likewise those of the land of Kefti (perhaps Crete) with their curly hair and long braids across their breasts. Then there are the black Africans of Kush, dressed in panther skins, who bring a jaguar, a giraffe, and monkeys, and the ambassadors of the land of Retenu (Syrians and Assyrians), who lead two horses, a bear, and an elephant.

The left wall of the corridor: a group of workers portrayed while sculpting a colossal statue of the pharaoh.
Below, the garden with workers caring for fruit trees around a central pond.

The Tomb of Userhat

Userhat, a royal scribe under Amenhotep II, had his tomb built and decorated with *paintings* which are still extraordinarily well preserved today. The unusual scene of a barber shaving his customer in a garden is famous.

Facing page, a group of servants paying homage to their master and men pulling on the bridle of a horse. Above, detail of a rowing boat.
Left and below, an unusual scene showing a barber.
A highly popular figure, the barber generally worked in the street, but when he shaved the nobles and aristocracy he visited them in their houses.

The Tomb of Khaemhet

Khaemhet, also known as Mahu, was a royal scribe and inspector of the granaries of Upper and Lower Egypt under Amenhotep III. His tomb, decorated with fine bas-reliefs, is at the end of a court surrounded by other tombs of the same period. In the niche of the burial chamber, dug deep into the rock, are statues of the deceased and his relations, divided into three groups.

Rather poorly preserved, these statues of Khaemhet and his relation Imhotep, a royal scribe, are located in a niche in the first large room of the tomb.

The Tomb of Neferhabef

Neferhabef, also called Userhat, was the First Prophet of the Royal Ka of Tuthmosis I at the time of the pharaoh Seti I. The goddess Isis appears in the decoration of the first room, in the form of a sycamore tree that nourishes the family of the deceased. The sycamore, together with the date palm, was the sacred tree which symbolized universal power.

Two priests in the act of making libations and offerings to the deities. The effeminate features of the men recall the art of Amarna.

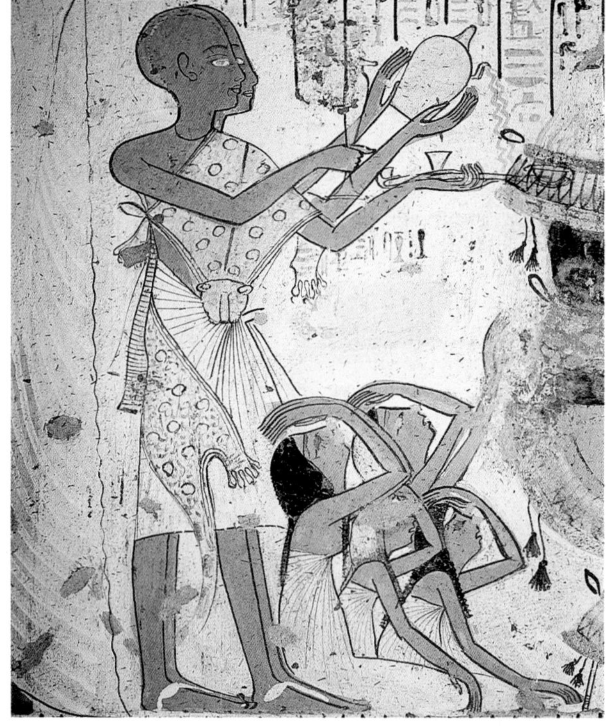

The Tomb of Ramose

The tomb of Ramose, Governor of Thebes and vizier under Amenhotep III and later Akhenaton, is a splendid example of the delicate moment of transition in Egyptian art toward the new Amarna style. The tomb was never finished, since during its construction the capital was moved from Thebes to Amarna, but the decoration that has remained intact - mainly bas-relief engravings - is quite splendid.

Husband and wife at table wearing heavy curled wigs, and two moments during the funeral procession, with mourners and servants carrying the furnishings.

The Tomb of Nakht

This tomb, typical of the 18th Dynasty, is one of the best preserved in the necropolis. The owner was a scribe and astronomer of Amun in the time of Tuthmosis IV, while his wife was a singer of Amun. At the time of Akhenaton's heresy, the name of Amun was systematically scratched out of all the inscriptions.
The appearance of the tomb is that of a classic hypogeum; the sophisticated decoration is found only in the transverse vestibule.

Facing page, work in the fields showing the reaping and gathering of corn, farm labourers tossing the ears of corn into the air to separate the seed from the husk, and treading the grapes.
This page, a kneeling servant offering flowers and a vine laden with bunches of grapes. Below, a large number of birds being prepared for the table.

The Tomb of Menna

The owner of this tomb was Menna, scribe of the Land Registry under Tuthmosis IV. To create it, he requisitioned - and enlarged - an earlier tomb. The brilliant paintings that embellish its walls with detailed, lively scenes are generally considered to be some of the most elegant in the whole necropolis and depict scenes of hunting and farming.

Above, a scene that is part of the cycle of agricultural work.

Right, two young girls dressed in light linen tunics bearing a jar of perfume and a bunch of lotus flowers and papyrus in offering.

Below, a detail of the scene of Menna hunting in the marshes, shown with his young daughter seated between his legs.

Opposite page: the vases carried by the woman as an offering to the deities are painted in a magnificent shade of blue. Below, during a reception at home, a woman offers the couple a necklace from which the ankh cross hangs, while pouring perfume onto the hands of the husband.

The Tomb of Nebamun and Ipuky

This tomb was prepared for two sculptors, both active under Amenhotep III and Amenhotep IV. Nebamun was Chief Sculptor of the Master of the Two Lands; Ipuky was Sculptor of the Master of the Two Lands. Known also as the tomb of the engravers, its interesting decoration shows much about how the artisans of ancient Egypt worked.

The deceased are purfied before being entombed; standing before the mummies of the two men is the widow who had married both the sculptors.

The Tomb of Kiki

The tomb of Kiki, "Superintendent of the Animals in the Temple of Amun", was long abandoned and even used as stables. Its decoration is brilliant and lively in both subject matter and execution. An entire wall is dedicated to scenes of the journey of the dead to Abydos. All Egyptians were required to make a pilgrimage to the temple of this sacred city, dedicated entirely to the worship of Osiris, at least once in their lifetime. Traditionally, Abydos was the sanctuary where the head of Osiris was preserved, and the greatest wish of all religious Egyptians was to have a mortuary chapel there - or at the very least a commemorative stele.

Kiki and his wife: the man is portrayed with a short beard and the woman carries a sistrum in her right hand.

These two images show the journey of the boat that accompanied the deceased to Abydos, with the wailing mourners, and a detail of the boat with the canopy beneath which lies the mummy of the deceased.

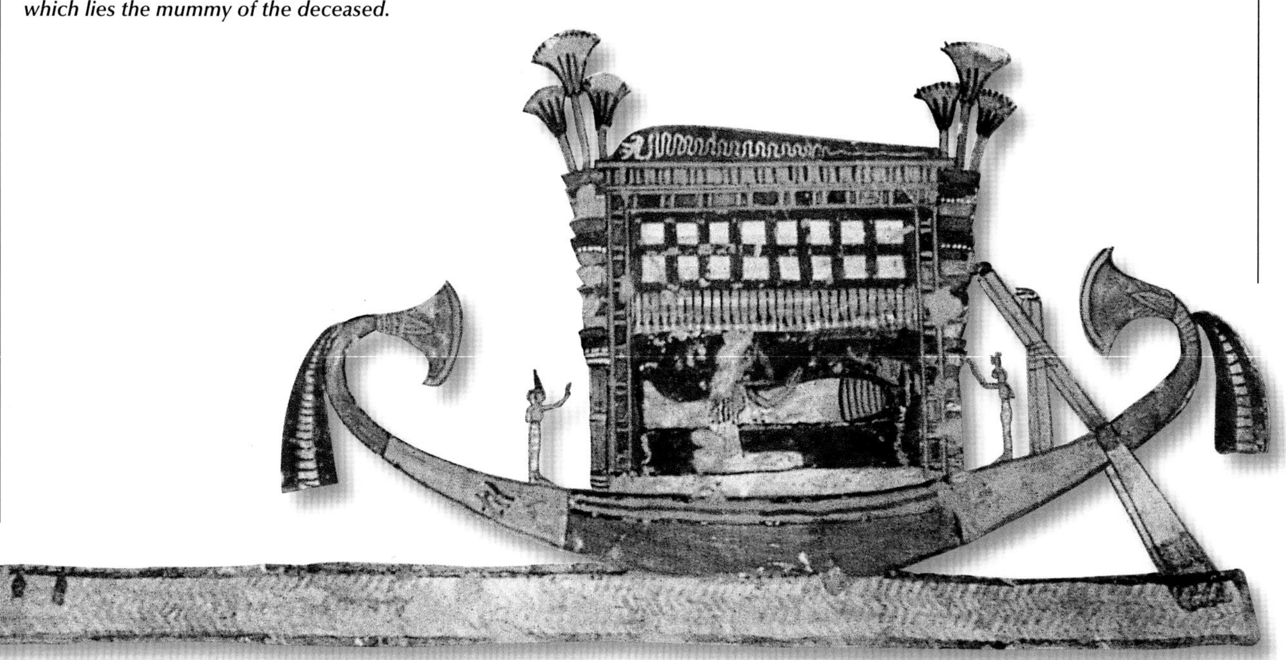

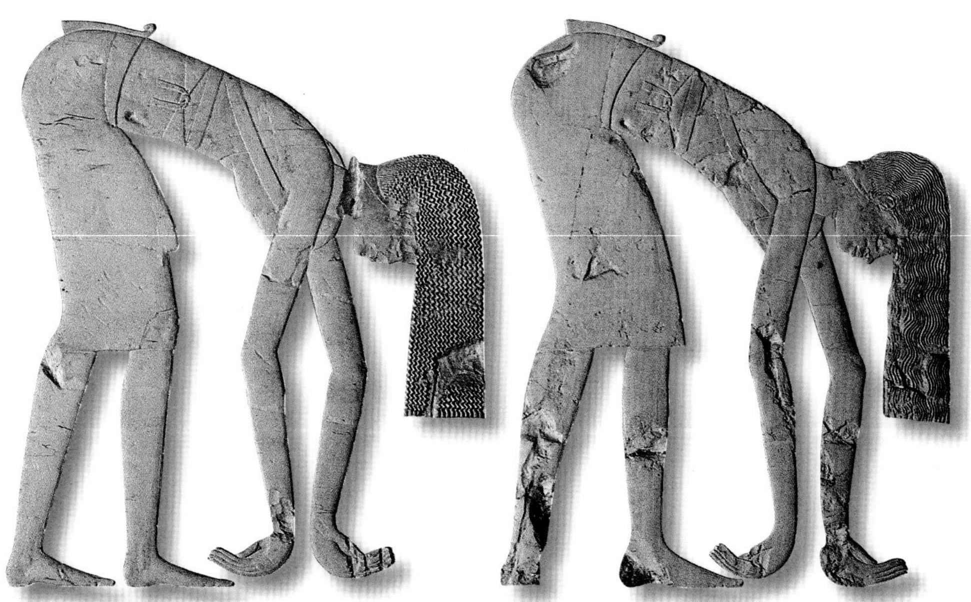

The Tomb of Kheruef Sena'a

Kheruef Sena'a was the "Superintendent of the Great Royal Bride", who was named Tiye, a Syrian princess famous for her beauty, the beloved wife of Amenhotep III and mother of Akhenaton, the heretic pharaoh.
The tomb the intendant had built is vast but unfinished. The western part of the court, with its depiction of Amenhotep III's Jubilee celebration (*Heb Sed*), is a true masterpiece.

The sophisticated engravings in this tomb illustrate young women conversing and dancing.

The Valley of the Artisans

A few kilometres south of Sheikh Abd al-Qurna, on the west bank of the Nile is the valley now known as Deir el-Medina, meaning "the Monastery of the Town" in Arabic, after a monastery that stood here during the Coptic period. Located here are the remains of a *village* that developed at the time of Amenhotep I where the workers who built and decorated the royal tombs of Thebes lived. This activity existed in the valley for five centuries from 1550 to 1000 BC, and the craftsmen who lived here were stone cutters, masons, painters, and sculptors, who every morning travelled the steep path over the harsh hills around Deir el-Bahri to the royal necropolis. The children and the women instead stayed in the village, where they cultivated wheat and barley. The workers laboured at the royal necropolis eight hours a day for nine consecutive days, and on the tenth - the day of rest - they decorated their own tombs. The teams of artisans (called Servants of the Place of Truth) were directed by several overseers and were divided into two groups: those who worked on the right walls and those who worked on the left.
As adepts of the royal tombs, these workers were considered "holders of secrets" and therefore subject to live in a village surrounded by walls.
The houses of the artisans were small and very simple: built one next to the other, in mud brick, they were whitewashed inside. Generally, they consisted of a tiny entrance, a reception room, a second room, and the kitchen. Sometimes, though infrequently, there was also a kitchen and terrace. Although very probably decorated, no trace of this has remained. The necropolis is on the west side of the valley. The tombs consisted of a chapel and a small underground painted chamber.

A view of the village from above. The necropolis extends across the hill to the west of the village. The Egyptians called it "Pa-demi", meaning the "Small town".

Peshedu kneeling beneath a dum palm tree and drinking the water of the Nile. The text in the background is Chapter 26 of the Book of the Dead, with the formula for drinking water in the Afterlife.

Right, the falcon Horus, portrayed with the Western mountain in the background, while an arm bearing a jar with a torch emerges from the eye. Osiris is represented wearing a nemes and his face is painted green.

Below, some of those who participated in the funeral of Peshedu: the father Menna, mother Huy and Nefersekheru, a friend of the deceased.

The Tomb of Peshedu

This tomb, from the Ramesside era, is located high up in the central sector of the necropolis. A steep staircase leads to the subterranean apartment, in which an unadorned antechamber precedes the *burial chamber*, with its mud brick walls covered with stucco and painted with tempera.
Peshedu is shown with his wife Nediem-behedet and his sons, and is referred to as a Servant of the Place of Truth – that is, a simple worker at the royal necropolis. As an older man, Peshedu was perhaps promoted to the level of foreman.
Only recently opened to visitors, the tomb is of interest not only for the lively, brilliant colours of its wall decorations, but also for the spiritual and religious significance of the verses of the *Book of the Dead* (*Am-Tuat*) they contain.

The wall at the back of the tomb with Sennedjem and his wife worshipping the gods of the Afterworld. In the lunette above, two figures of Anubis protect the doors of the next world.

THE TOMB OF SENNEDJEM

In the vivacity and freshness of its decoration, the tomb of Sennedjem, "Servant of the Place of Truth" and an official of the necropolis in the 19th Dynasty, is perhaps the finest to be found here. All that remains of it is the main burial chamber though this is almost perfectly intact; the furnishings that it held are now on exhibit in the Egyptian Museum of Cairo.

On the opposite page, a famous image of Osiris, his body wrapped in a shroud, hands and face painted green to symbolise the renascent vegetation. In his hands he carries the pastoral and flail and on his head is the atef crown.

This page, an image of Lyneferti, wife of Sennedjem. On her head is a cone of solid perfume which releases a pleasant fragrance as it melts.

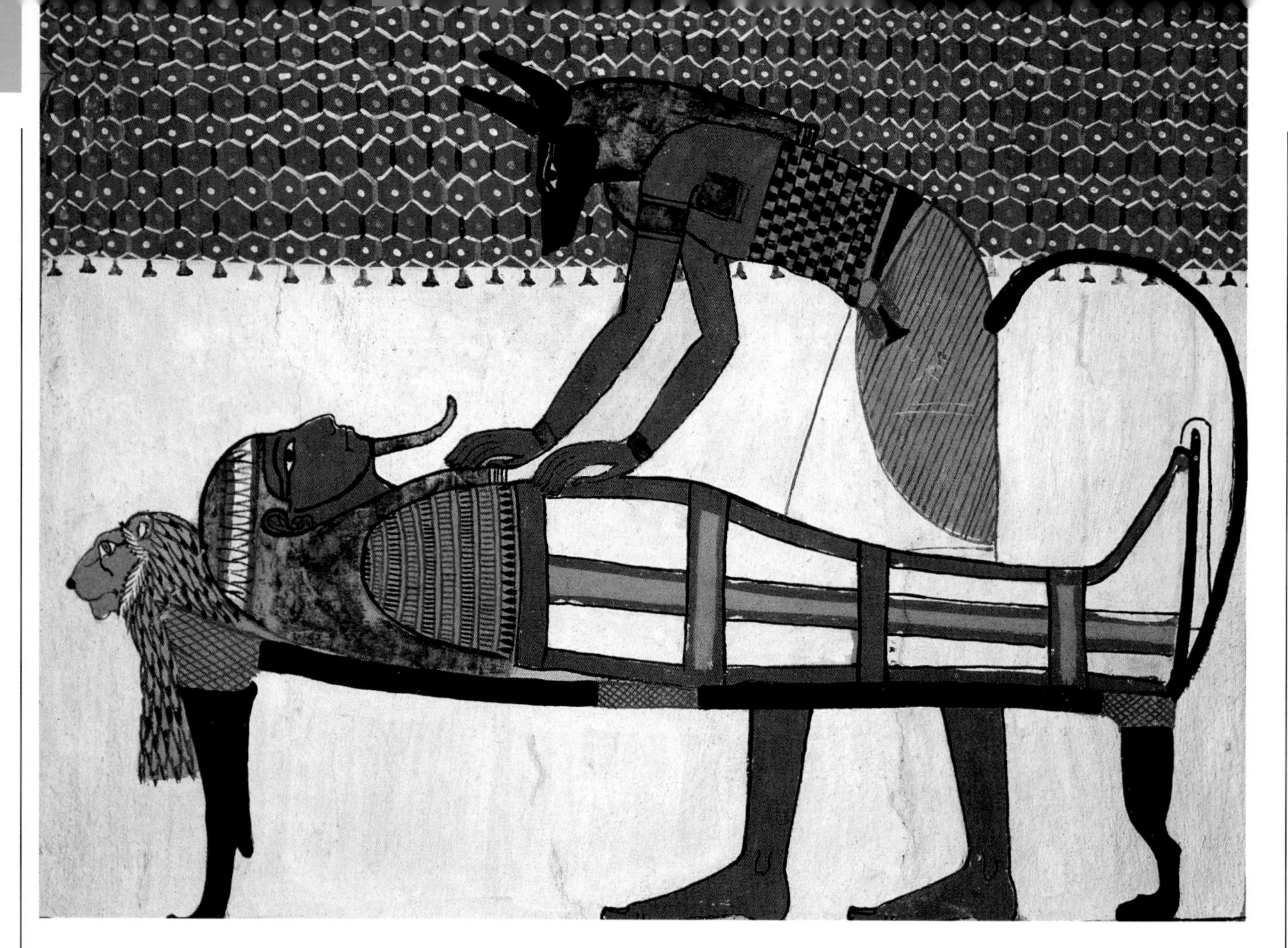

One of the most important moments of the funeral rites is illustrated on a wall of Sennedjem's tomb, as the priest, wearing a mask of Anubis, touches the heart and stomach of the mummy to awaken and accompany him to the Afterlife.

This delightful scene of rural life is also in the tomb of Sennedjem. The deceased is represented reaping with the typical Egyptian scythe which has a short wooden handle, followed by his wife who gathers the fallen ears of the crop.

The Tomb of Anherkhe

Under Ramesses III and Ramesses IV, Anherkhe held the office of "Chief of the Team of the Lord of the Two Lands in the Place of Truth"; he was, in other words, a foreman, entrusted with coordinating the work of the labourers under his direction. He had two tombs built for himself, but only the one lower down the slope, closer to the village, has lively, imaginative decoration.

Details of the painted decoration in the tomb of Anherkhe: the procession (above), a scarab with a Hathor necklace (centre) and the solar boat sailing in the Underworld (right), with the deceased preceded by Isis, Thoth, Khepri and Hu.

More splendid images in the tomb of Anherkhe: left, the elegant stride of four slender Anubis and below, three genies with the heads of jackals.

The Tomb of Ipy

Ipy, a sculptor under Ramesses II, had his tomb decorated with unusual and curious scenes: even if the style is rather sketchy, the wealth of detail (for example, the oculist putting drops into the eyes of a patient) is such as to make this one of the best-known tombs in the necropolis.

A painting on plaster in the tomb of Ipy illustrating a fishing scene in the marshes using nets and the traditional light papyrus boat.

The Temple of Deir el-Medina

The Small Temple at Deir el-Medina, dedicated to the deities of the necropolis, Hathor and Ma'at, was begun by Ptolemy IV Philopator and completed under Euergetes II. Later occupied by Christian monks, the temple has survived complete with its enclosing walls and storehouses. On the rear wall, decorated near the top with seven masks of Hathor, are three chapels with beautiful ornamental reliefs.

The simple façade of the Ptolemaic temple and below, the temple in a drawing by David Roberts.

Editorial project: Casa Editrice Bonechi
Editorial management: Giovanna Magi
Graphic design: Manuela Ranfagni
Video layout: Teresa Donato
Cover: Manuela Ranfagni
Picture research: Giovanna Magi
Texts: Giovanna Magi
Editor: Patrizia Fabbri
Translation and revision of English texts: Eve Leckey
Drawings on pages 12, 24-25, 32, 35, 36-37, 40, 49, 58, 71: Stefano Benini
Drawings on page 41 above: Sauro Giampaia

E-mail: bonechi@bonechi.it

Printed in Italy by Centro Stampa Editoriale Bonechi.

The photographs belong to the archive of Casa Editrice Bonechi, and were taken by
Marco Bonechi, Marco Carpi Ceci, Michael Clears, Emanuela Crimini, Luigi Di Giovine, Paolo Giambone, Andrea Pistolesi, Mario Tosi.

Other archives:
Gianni Dagli Orti: pp. 18 above, 38, 39, 40 (photos relating to the drawing, clockwise from left: the second, third and fourth), 41 below, 42, 43 (all photos, except below), 44 left, 46, 47 above and below left, 48, 49 below, 50, 51 (all photos except above right), 52 below right, 63 below, 74 above, 76 above, 82 above, 94 above and below.
Getty Images by Laura Ronchi: pp. 3 below, 5, 12 above.
Andrea Jemolo: pp. 16/17 above and below, 18/19 above and below, 40 above and the first photo of the drawing, left, 41 above right.

The publisher apologises for any omissions and is willing to make amends if informed by the relevant rights holders.

ISBN 978-88-476-1914-2

www.bonechi.com

* * *